# BASEBALL INTELLECT

# BASEBALL INTELLECT

## 101 Inside Tips for Players, Fans and Coaches

Larry Downes and D. Bruce Gilbert

**Canadian Cataloguing in Publication Data**

Downes, Larry, 1960–
    Baseball intellect : 101 inside tips for players,
fans and coaches

ISBN 0-7710-2830-X

1. Baseball.  I Gilbert, D. Bruce (Devin Bruce), 1957–
II. Title

GV867.D68  1995        796.357        C95–930686–2


Printed and bound in Canada. The paper used in this book is acid-free.

McClelland & Stewart Inc
*The Canadian Publishers*
481 University Avenue
Toronto, Ontario
M5G 2E9

1  2  3  4  5   99  98  97  96  95

To Jim and Mary

"This is a simple game. You throw the ball, you catch the ball,

you hit the ball."

– from the motion picture *Bull Durham*

# Foreword

In baseball at the major-league level, there are different degrees of success depending on the individual player's dedication to his career and on whether he has an understanding of what it takes to be a champion. All players have more or less the same physical skills. Sure, there are players who run faster, throw harder and hit the ball farther, but once a player has made it into the major leagues, he has already established himself as having the tools to perform at that level. The difference, then, between a major-league player and a champion is, to my mind, his "baseball intellect."

Paul Molitor no longer has the same physical skills that he had when he played for the Milwaukee Brewers in his first year, but he has worked on the mental aspects of the game to maintain the edge that separates him from most of the players he broke in with. He has tremendous baseball intellect. Molitor can gain an edge just by watching, as the game progresses, an opposing pitcher's patterns and using that information later in the game to deliver a clutch hit. He runs the bases as if he knows what's going to happen before the play unfolds because he checks to see who is playing the defensive positions and asks himself how do they throw? Do they have the speed to cut off the ball in the gap? Does the shortstop tense up in pressured situations? All of these characteristics are right there for everyone to judge and put to good use, but it's only players like Molitor, those with a keen baseball intellect, who think to ask the questions and use the answers in his game. It is no fluke that Paul Molitor is closing in on 3,000 career hits. He has worked diligently to understand what he can do to maximize his physical skills.

I single out Paul Molitor because we were teammates in Milwaukee when he first came up in the early 1970s and I am able to watch him again on a daily basis while broadcasting Blue Jays games on television. I marvel at the way he is able to maintain such a high level of performance during the waning years of his career. But he is by no means the only player with baseball intellect. When you see a player, a coach or a manager enjoying all-star careers and championship seasons, you can bet that he has put more than practice alone into his game preparation. He has limbered up his baseball intellect on a regular basis and has used it to be the best.

Buck Martinez

## Preface

I go to major-league baseball games a lot, and I am often surprised by what I overhear spectators saying to each other as they watch the game. Most appear to know the fundamentals of baseball, but only a few seem to be able to appreciate the various offensive and defensive strategies being played out in front of them. I admit that I get annoyed when the crowd grows restless when a game remains scoreless inning after inning because a great pitchers' duel is being played out on the field. I have to remind myself that I am fortunate in knowing many of the subtle strategies of the game and that most fans never get the chance to learn them.

I started to write the "Baseball Intellect" strip so that anyone who wanted to learn and to appreciate the subtle nuances and the finer mental aspects of the game as it is played at the major-league level could do so. And the response from readers of *Baseball Weekly,* which publishes "Baseball Intellect" has been very encouraging. Not only have many of them written to thank me for the strip, but many have also asked when I would put the strips together as a book. The publishers McClelland & Stewart also thought there was a book in the strips. And now you are holding it.

I hope that *Baseball Intellect* will help improve players' games. For slow-pitch players and aspiring professionals alike, understanding the subtleties of the game can only improve their performance. Coaches may learn a few hints on how to communicate to their players in the pages of this book. As for fans, *Baseball Intellect* should help them appreciate the game even more and add to their baseball intellect.

In closing, I want to thank Bruce Gilbert for his efforts and abilities in drawing each strip. Thanks also to Therese, my wife, who never played an inning but showed me how to be a winner. And many thanks to David, Paul, Greg, Larry and Baseball Canada who all encouraged me to do "Baseball Intellect." Finally, thanks to all the players and coaches I've had the privilege to play with.

Larry Downes

# Contents

**Hitting**

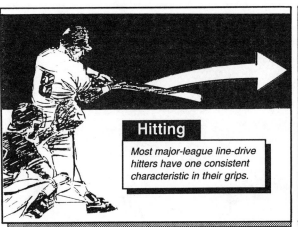

## Hitting

*Most major-league line-drive hitters have one consistent characteristic in their grips.*

*At the instant the bat makes contact with the ball, they have their top hand directly behind the bat and their bottom hand directly in front of it. Once contact is made the top hand begins to roll over the bottom hand. This grip is a vital part of a good line-drive swing.*

3

## Hitting

*Hitters usually have about one-fifth of a second to decide whether to swing at a pitch, so it is vital that they "pick up" the ball from the pitcher's hand as soon as possible.*

*Good hitters focus on the pitcher's cap emblem because his throwing arm will come out from behind his head. With a sidearm pitcher, the hitter focuses on the pitcher's belt buckle because his throwing arm will come out from behind his hip.*

4

## Hitting

In an effort to increase the power of his swing, the hitter will strive for maximum arm extension. If properly executed, the hitter will form "the hitting triangle" just after contact.

The triangle constitutes both arms fully extended toward the bat and the hitter's head tucked between his shoulders.

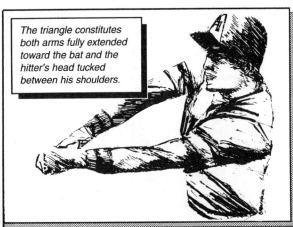

## Hitting

*In the early part of the season, some major-league hitters struggle at the plate because they are lunging at the ball. In a fundamentally sound swing, the hips and lower body come forward first, followed by the hands.*

*When the hitter lunges, his hips and hands come forward at the same time. This improper alignment shifts all his weight to his front foot and eliminates most of his power.*

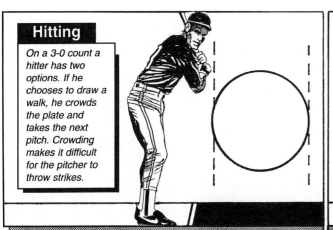

## Hitting

*On a 3-0 count a hitter has two options. If he chooses to draw a walk, he crowds the plate and takes the next pitch. Crowding makes it difficult for the pitcher to throw strikes.*

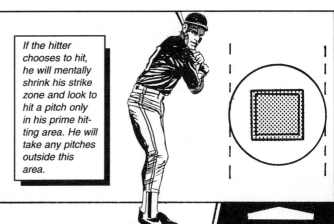

*If the hitter chooses to hit, he will mentally shrink his strike zone and look to hit a pitch only in his prime hitting area. He will take any pitches outside this area.*

## Hitting

A good hitter constantly studies the pitcher to detect certain pitching patterns like first-pitch fastballs. A pitcher may even telegraph his intention by movements like breathing deeply before throwing a fastball.

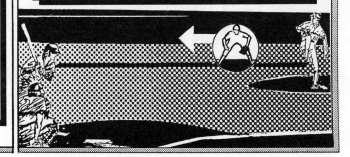

Behind the pitcher, an infielder or catcher may also tip off a pitch by shifting during the pitcher's wind-up. Exploiting these idiosyncrasies can turn a .250 hitter into a .280 hitter.

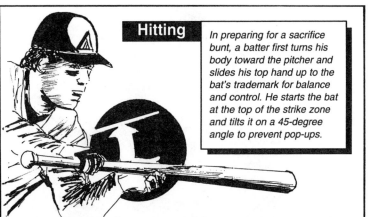

## Hitting

*In preparing for a sacrifice bunt, a batter first turns his body toward the pitcher and slides his top hand up to the bat's trademark for balance and control. He starts the bat at the top of the strike zone and tilts it on a 45-degree angle to prevent pop-ups.*

*Finally, as the ball approaches, he maintains his eye level on the same plane as his bat by bending his knees.*

9

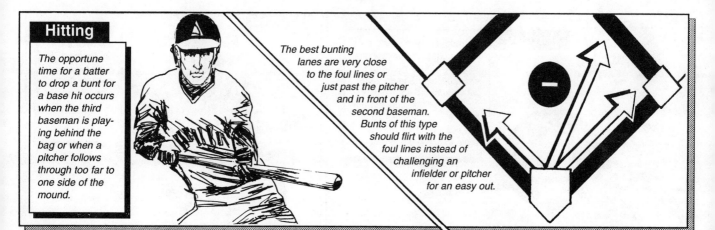

## Hitting

*The opportune time for a batter to drop a bunt for a base hit occurs when the third baseman is playing behind the bag or when a pitcher follows through too far to one side of the mound.*

*The best bunting lanes are very close to the foul lines or just past the pitcher and in front of the second baseman. Bunts of this type should flirt with the foul lines instead of challenging an infielder or pitcher for an easy out.*

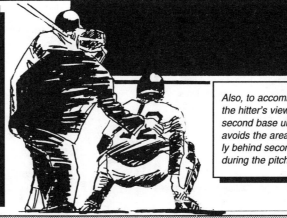

In most major-league stadiums, the background directly behind the pitcher is an expanse of black or green. This area has no spectators, signs or cameras and so gives the hitter the best possible background to see the pitched ball.

Also, to accommodate the hitter's view, the second base umpire avoids the area directly behind second base during the pitch.

## Hitting

*A skilled pitcher constantly searches the ball for its highest seam. By working his fingers off this seam he can gain the maximum amount of spin on his breaking pitches.*

*Similarly, a good hitter will search for a bat with the widest grain. This allows the maximum surface area to make contact with the ball. Also, a wide-grained bat is less susceptible to cracking and chipping.*

**Infielding**

## Fielding

*Major-league infielders are taught "always play the ball, don't let the ball play you." This refers to getting into proper position to field a ground ball at its short hop.*

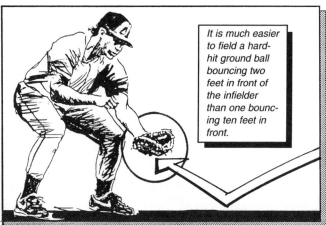

*It is much easier to field a hard-hit ground ball bouncing two feet in front of the infielder than one bouncing ten feet in front.*

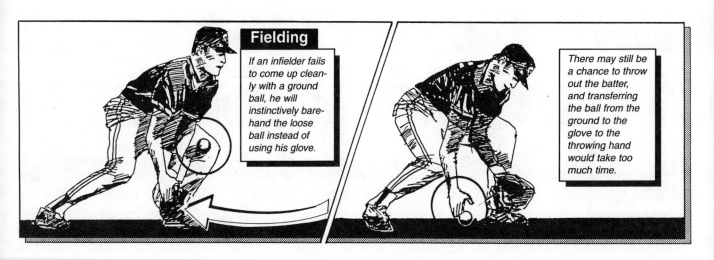

## Fielding

*If an infielder fails to come up cleanly with a ground ball, he will instinctively bare-hand the loose ball instead of using his glove.*

*There may still be a chance to throw out the batter, and transferring the ball from the ground to the glove to the throwing hand would take too much time.*

16

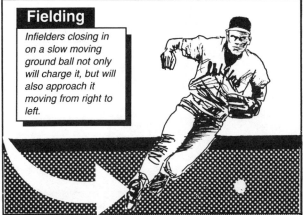

## Fielding

*Infielders closing in on a slow moving ground ball not only will charge it, but will also approach it moving from right to left.*

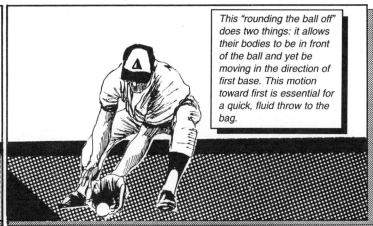

*This "rounding the ball off" does two things: it allows their bodies to be in front of the ball and yet be moving in the direction of first base. This motion toward first is essential for a quick, fluid throw to the bag.*

## Fielding

*High pop-ups behind first and third base are the responsibility of the middle infielders.*

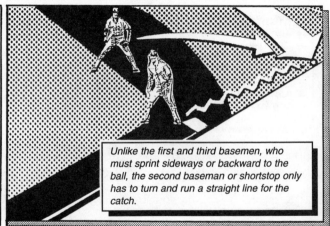

*Unlike the first and third basemen, who must sprint sideways or backward to the ball, the second baseman or shortstop only has to turn and run a straight line for the catch.*

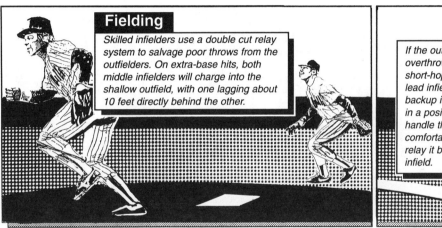

## Fielding

*Skilled infielders use a double cut relay system to salvage poor throws from the outfielders. On extra-base hits, both middle infielders will charge into the shallow outfield, with one lagging about 10 feet directly behind the other.*

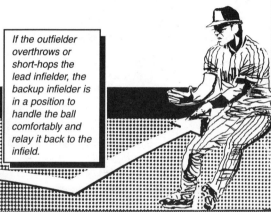

*If the outfielder overthrows or short-hops the lead infielder, the backup infielder is in a position to handle the ball comfortably and relay it back to the infield.*

## Fielding

On any attempted pickoff play at first base, the shortstop should instinctively move toward second base.

In the event that the runner breaks toward second base, the shortstop is responsible for covering the bag on a throw from the first baseman. Usually, the second baseman is too far away to get involved in the play at second.

## Fielding

*On a routine ground ball hit to an infielder, the first baseman must identify the direction of the infielder's throw before he begins his body stretch toward the ball.*

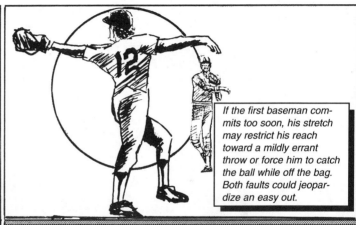

*If the first baseman commits too soon, his stretch may restrict his reach toward a mildly errant throw or force him to catch the ball while off the bag. Both faults could jeopardize an easy out.*

21

## Fielding

*On a double play, the pivot man will always try to catch the lead toss with two hands for balance, fluency and a quick transfer and release. He does not drag his throwing arm.*

*As well, he will push off with his right leg to finish the throw and to initiate his leap over the sliding runner.*

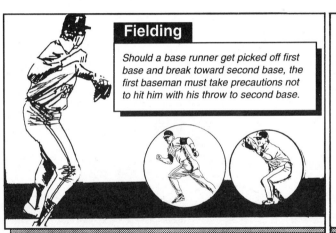

## Fielding

*Should a base runner get picked off first base and break toward second base, the first baseman must take precautions not to hit him with his throw to second base.*

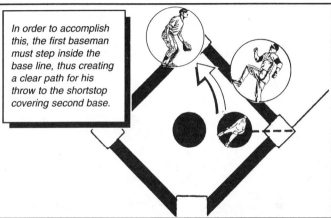

*In order to accomplish this, the first baseman must step inside the base line, thus creating a clear path for his throw to the shortstop covering second base.*

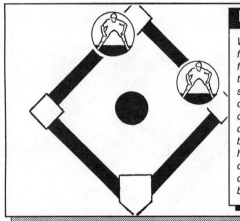

## Fielding

With runners on first and second, fewer than two out, the third baseman starts a ground ball double play in the direction the ball carries him. On balls hit to his left, he throws to second base to begin a conventional double play.

On balls hit to his right, he steps on third base, forcing out the lead runner, and then throws to first base to retire the batter. This is the easiest double play.

24

**Outfielding**

## Fielding

A skilled outfielder catching a routine fly ball with men on base and fewer than two out will catch it over his throwing shoulder.

This way, if the runners try to tag up and advance, the outfielder's arm is already cocked to throw the ball to the appropriate base.

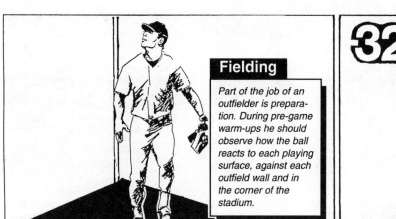

### Fielding

Part of the job of an outfielder is preparation. During pre-game warm-ups he should observe how the ball reacts to each playing surface, against each outfield wall and in the corner of the stadium.

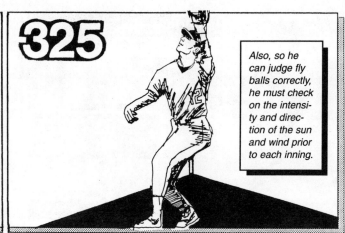

**325**

Also, so he can judge fly balls correctly, he must check on the intensity and direction of the sun and wind prior to each inning.

28

## Fielding

High fly balls near the fence are very difficult to catch. Not only is the outfielder faced with playing the ball, he must also contend with locating the barrier.

Once in contact with the fence, he can focus on one thing: catching the ball.

## Fielding

*A good defensive outfielder has the ability to locate and catch line drives. On line drives hit straight at him, he knows he must freeze momentarily until he judges whether the ball is hit behind or in front of him. He must not commit too soon.*

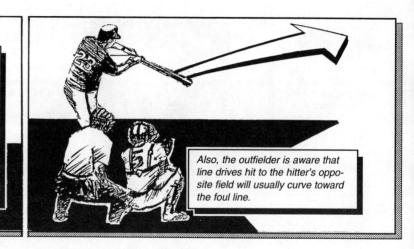

*Also, the outfielder is aware that line drives hit to the hitter's opposite field will usually curve toward the foul line.*

## Fielding

*On short fly balls just over the infield, the incoming outfielder has priority over the outgoing infielder. In most cases, the outfielder is in a much better position to make the catch since he is running toward the ball.*

*Also, since he is moving toward the infield, he can quickly throw the ball to the appropriate base, if necessary.*

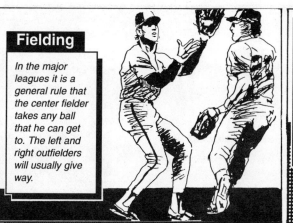

## Fielding

In the major leagues it is a general rule that the center fielder takes any ball that he can get to. The left and right outfielders will usually give way.

Another rule involves balls hit in the gap, when the fastest outfielder will cut in front of the slower outfielder in a effort to get to the ball quicker. These rules are designed to prevent head-on collisions.

## Fielding

*In major-league stadiums with deep power alleys, the right and left outfielders will play closer to the center fielder instead of playing straight away. This is called "playing the gaps."*

**395**

*Usually, any ball hit into the corner is a sure double, no matter where the outfielders play. However, deep power alleys must be protected since balls hit here may result in a triple.*

## Fielding

In a relay throw, the cutoff man should be in a straight line between the outfielder and the base where the runner is headed. The outfielder's throw should cover 60 per cent of the distance to the base; the infielder's, the remaining 40 per cent.

Based on this ratio, most teams put their best arm in right field, since throws from there to third base or home plate are two of the longest throws in the game.

34

The way major-league ballparks are built, the right fielder and left fielder often must contend with the sun or a bank of lights shining in their eyes while catching a high fly ball.

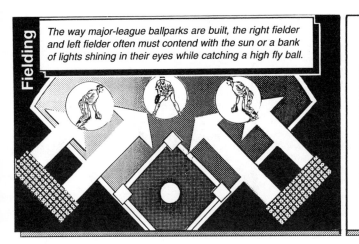

To remedy the situation, some fielders will turn sideways to catch a high fly ball, thus avoiding direct contact with the sun or lights.

## Fielding

When a fast base runner on first base is easily advancing to third on a base hit, the outfielder should concede to the runner and throw the ball to second base. The priority here is to keep the batter out of scoring position.

This same strategy is used when the bases are loaded on a deep sacrifice fly ball out. The outfielder should concede the run and instead try to prevent the runner at second base from tagging up and advancing to third base.

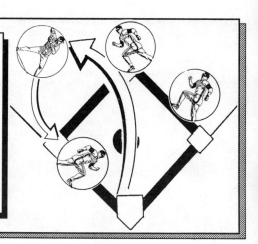

36

**Pitching**

## Pitching

*A right hander should start his wind-up while standing on the right side of the pitching rubber. This causes his pitch to come in on an angle toward the plate instead of just over the top.*

*This delivery can sometimes intimidate the right-handed batter and cause him to shy away from the pitch, just enough to throw off his swing.*

## Pitching

*Balance is the pitcher's key to accuracy and control. At the top of his leg kick the pitcher positions both shoulders directly over his pivot leg. They are not tipped back.*

*Also, at this point in his delivery, his hip pocket is pointed toward the plate.*

## Pitching

*Throwing across the body is one mechanical reason why a pitcher may develop a streak of wildness during the game. This flaw involves the pitcher's stride-leg landing too far toward his throwing side, thus causing his arm to throw across an off-center fulcrum.*

*By striding more toward the plate and in line with the center of his body, the pitcher will be more accurate and save much wear and tear on his arm.*

## Pitching

*In major-league base-ball an effective fast-ball has three charac-teristics. First, it has velocity in excess of 85 miles per hour. Second, it has good location, preferably thrown low at the knees or high on the hands, and on the cor-ners of the plate.*

*Finally, the fastball has movement, the apparent ability to explode a couple of inches up, down, left or right just before reach-ing the plate.*

## Pitching

*During the course of a nine-inning game, a pitcher may experience a temporary bout of pitching too high. One possible correction the pitching coach or catcher may offer is a deeper bend of the back knee during the pitcher's wind-up.*

*This slight mechanical adjustment lowers the pitcher's body and throwing arm. It means he can deliver the pitch at a lower level toward the plate for a strike.*

43

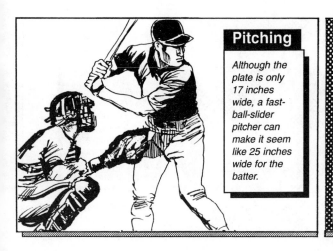

## Pitching

*Although the plate is only 17 inches wide, a fast-ball-slider pitcher can make it seem like 25 inches wide for the batter.*

*When the pitcher runs a fastball in on the batter's hands and then strings a slider out on the outside corner, the batter cannot prepare effectively to cover both parts of the plate to hit the ball well. This creates the illusion of a very wide plate.*

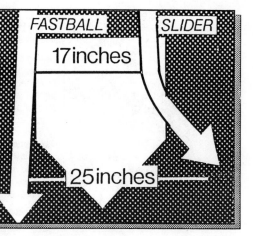

FASTBALL    SLIDER

17 inches

25 inches

## Pitching

There is a vast difference between a pitcher deliberately throwing at a batter and establishing himself inside. Throwing at a batter is dangerous, against the rules and unsportsmanlike.

Establishing himself inside means throwing the ball at the inside corner, or farther in, to back the hitter off the plate. This strategy can throw off the hitter's swing and make him vulnerable to pitches on the outside corner later in the count.

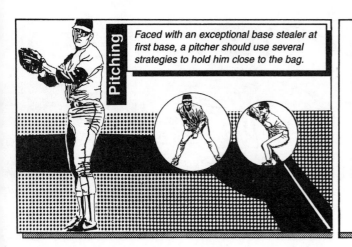

**Pitching**

*Faced with an exceptional base stealer at first base, a pitcher should use several strategies to hold him close to the bag.*

*Besides using two or three pickoff moves, the pitcher should vary the number of "looks" to both first base and home plate. He should also vary the interval between staying "set" and delivering the ball to first or home.*

## Pitching

*There are two maneuvers a left-handed pitcher uses to hold or pick off a runner at first base without balking. Initially, he balances his raised leg above an imaginary line from the pitching rubber to first base. From here, he can throw to either home plate or first base, thus "freezing" the runner.*

*Second, as his right stride leg moves toward home plate, he can still throw to first base provided his foot lands on the first base side of the area between first and home.*

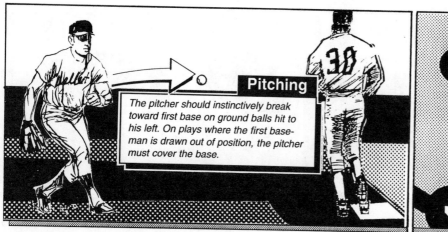

## Pitching

The pitcher should instinctively break toward first base on ground balls hit to his left. On plays where the first baseman is drawn out of position, the pitcher must cover the base.

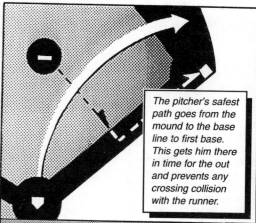

The pitcher's safest path goes from the mound to the base line to first base. This gets him there in time for the out and prevents any crossing collision with the runner.

## Pitching

*While holding a runner at second base, the pitcher must prevent him from taking a walking lead. This is done by varying the number of looks toward second base and/or by staring down the runner until he stops moving.*

*Also, should the middle infielders break toward the bag to keep the runner close, the pitcher must wait until they return to their positions before delivering the pitch. Otherwise he simply steps off the rubber.*

## Pitching

Late in the game, with runners at second and third, most major-league pitchers will pitch from the half wind-up instead of from the full wind-up.

This half wind-up will keep the runner at second base closer to the bag. On any ensuing base hit, he has to travel a greater distance to score, and the outfielder has a better chance of throwing him out at home plate.

## Pitching

*On a ground ball back to the mound with nobody out and runners on first and second, the pitcher must resist throwing to third base to start a double play.*

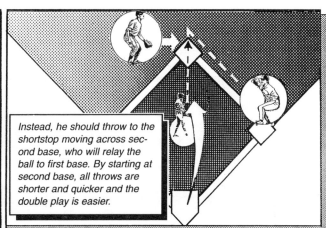

*Instead, he should throw to the shortstop moving across second base, who will relay the ball to first base. By starting at second base, all throws are shorter and quicker and the double play is easier.*

## Pitching

In a close game with no one out and runners in scoring position, the major-league pitcher knows that giving up any hard contact could score a run, or at least move up the runners. So, his strategy will focus on trying to strike the batter out.

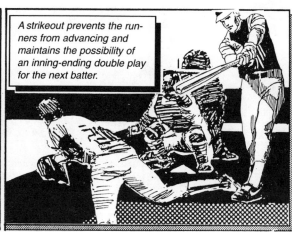

A strikeout prevents the runners from advancing and maintains the possibility of an inning-ending double play for the next batter.

## Pitching

On a hard-hit ball back to the mound, the pitcher should resist the temptation to stab at the ball with his bare pitching hand.

The slightest damage at all to the hand could force him to leave the game. Also, if the middle infielders have drawn a bead on the ball, any change of direction caused by the pitcher could jeopardize their chances of making a play on the ball.

**Catching**

## Catching

In an effort to communicate pitch selection and location to the pitcher, a catcher will use a series of finger and hand signals from behind the plate.

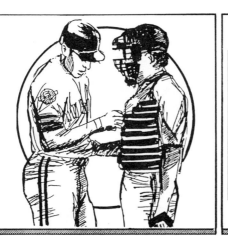

To avoid detection by the opposing team, the catcher gives the signal deep in his crotch area while the batter is looking at the pitcher. Also, he blocks the sightline of the opposing third base coach by placing his glove at his left knee.

## Catching

*As a rule, umpires set up for the pitch on the batter's side of home plate. Because of this, catchers will rarely position themselves on the inside corner. This inside position can obscure the umpire's view of the outside part of the plate. Also, the inside position can tip off the batter about the coming pitch's location and type.*

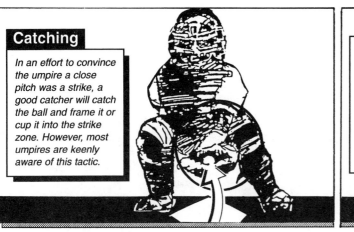

## Catching

*In an effort to convince the umpire a close pitch was a strike, a good catcher will catch the ball and frame it or cup it into the strike zone. However, most umpires are keenly aware of this tactic.*

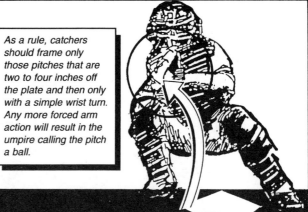

*As a rule, catchers should frame only those pitches that are two to four inches off the plate and then only with a simple wrist turn. Any more forced arm action will result in the umpire calling the pitch a ball.*

## Catching

*In an effort to gain a strike call, the catcher will "cut off" a breaking pitch just after it crosses the plate.*

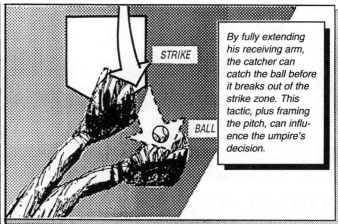

STRIKE

BALL

*By fully extending his receiving arm, the catcher can catch the ball before it breaks out of the strike zone. This tactic, plus framing the pitch, can influence the umpire's decision.*

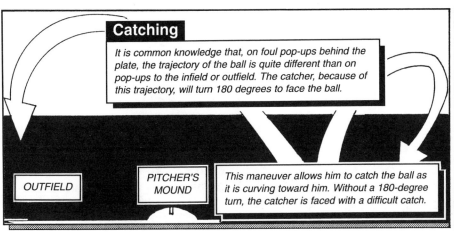

## Catching

*It is common knowledge that, on foul pop-ups behind the plate, the trajectory of the ball is quite different than on pop-ups to the infield or outfield. The catcher, because of this trajectory, will turn 180 degrees to face the ball.*

OUTFIELD

PITCHER'S MOUND

*This maneuver allows him to catch the ball as it is curving toward him. Without a 180-degree turn, the catcher is faced with a difficult catch.*

## Catching

*On a high pop-up the catcher will get to the ball while still carrying his mask.*

*This prevents him from tripping over it as he tracks the ball. Once he determines where the ball will come down, he discards the mask in the opposite direction.*

## Catching

In the major leagues, base stealers can steal second base in well under four seconds. To give the catcher a good shot at throwing out the runner, the pitcher must deliver the ball to the plate in 1.3 to 1.5 seconds.

Once the catcher receives the ball, he has from 1.9 to 2.3 seconds to get out of his crouch and make a strong, accurate throw to second base. There is not much room for error.

## Catching

On an attempted steal of second base with runners on first and third, the catcher must glance at the runner on third just before throwing to second base.

This glance prevents the runner at third from attempting to score on the long throw to second base. Also, the catcher can fake a throw to second base and try to pick off the runner at third.

## Catching

Usually, on a sacrifice bunt, the pitcher, third baseman or first baseman fields the ball. Since they cannot see the base runners, the catcher is responsible for instructing the fielder where to throw the ball.

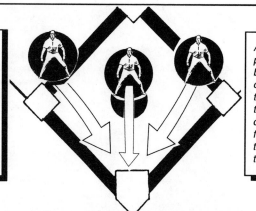

After judging the placement of the bunt, the progress of the runner and the progress of the fielder, the catcher alerts the fielder to throw out the lead runner or the batter.

**Running**

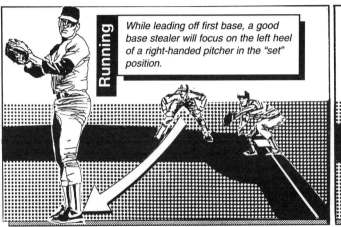

Running

While leading off first base, a good base stealer will focus on the left heel of a right-handed pitcher in the "set" position.

Lifting the left heel is the first movement a right-handed pitcher must make in delivering the ball to the plate. Once the left heel is raised, the good base stealer is off and running toward second base.

## Running

*Most skilled base stealers take a first base lead that measures their body length plus one step.*

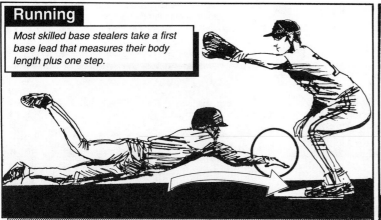

*On a pickoff, the quickest way back is head first. The arms extend toward the back side of the base, thus avoiding the tag, while the head turns toward foul territory for protection and to pick up a possible errant pickoff throw.*

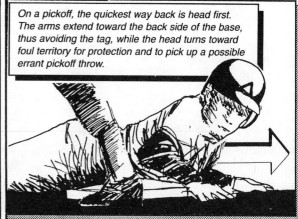

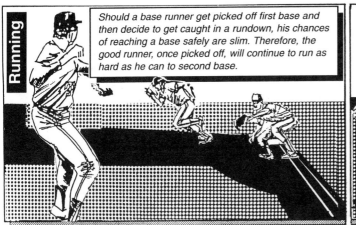

**Running**

Should a base runner get picked off first base and then decide to get caught in a rundown, his chances of reaching a base safely are slim. Therefore, the good runner, once picked off, will continue to run as hard as he can to second base.

This strategy is based on the runner's speed beating the first baseman's throw and/or the possibility of the ball hitting him on its way to second base.

## Running

The delayed steal is an offensive maneuver in which the base stealer breaks toward second base just as the pitch enters the catcher's glove.

The delayed steal is designed to capitalize on two things: first, a lazy catcher remaining too long in his crouch, thus hampering his throw; second, the two middle infielders haphazardly covering second base after the pitch.

## Running

During the heat of the game, an overly aggressive batter, in an effort to reach first base safely on a ground ball, will slide into first base.

With all due respect to the batter's intensity, the reason a player slides is to slow down. The fastest way to get to first base is not to slide but to continue running through the bag, as hard as possible.

## Running

While stealing second base, the skilled base runner will peek toward home plate during his fourth stride. At about this time, the ball enters the hitting zone and the runner can identify where the ball is headed.

If caught running blindly, he is susceptible to line-drive double plays or to the defense decoying him into stopping or sliding at second base on an extra-base hit.

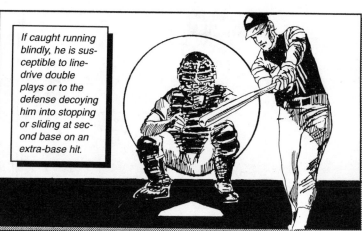

## Running

A good base runner will take a walking lead off third base in foul territory. He is keenly aware that if a batted ball hits him in fair territory, he is called out.

When returning to third base after a pitch, the base runner will come back in fair territory, thus obscuring the catcher's view of third and discouraging him from an attempted pickoff.

With fewer than two out, good base runners will "freeze" or tag up on line drives. They know that infielders who snare a line drive can easily double them off.

On a line drive hit to the outfield, any attempt to advance after a catch is thwarted if the base runner fails to "freeze" or tag up and is instead caught in the middle of the base line.

## Running

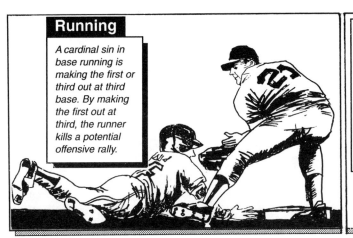

A cardinal sin in base running is making the first or third out at third base. By making the first out at third, the runner kills a potential offensive rally.

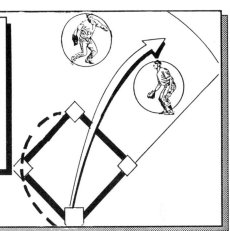

By making the third out at third, the runner not only ends the inning, but also removes himself from scoring position at second base. Had he remained at second, he could have easily scored on an ensuring base hit.

## Running

When caught in a rundown, a skilled base runner has two aims. The first is to remain in the rundown long enough to allow other base runners to move up a base.

Second, he will try to run into a defensive player and hope for an interference call by the umpire.

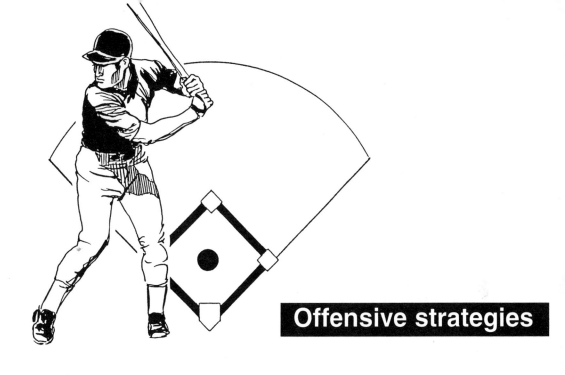

**Offensive strategies**

## Offense

*A batter has three priorities in executing a proper hit and run. Since the runner is breaking on the pitch, the batter must make contact with the ball. Second, he tries to hit the ball on the ground, thus avoiding a fly ball or line-drive double play.*

*Finally, if possible, the batter tries to hit the ball in the direction of the spot that the middle infielder vacated to cover the attempted steal.*

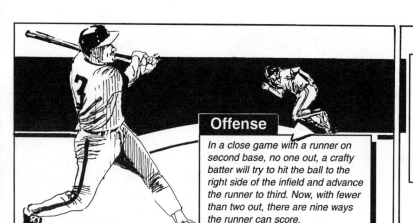

## Offense

*In a close game with a runner on second base, no one out, a crafty batter will try to hit the ball to the right side of the infield and advance the runner to third. Now, with fewer than two out, there are nine ways the runner can score.*

*To counter this offensive strategy, a good pitcher will try to pitch a right-handed batter on the inside corner or a left-handed batter on the outside corner.*

## Offense

*One way a major-league manager can maximize the efforts of his best fastball hitter is to slot him behind his best base stealer in the batting order.*

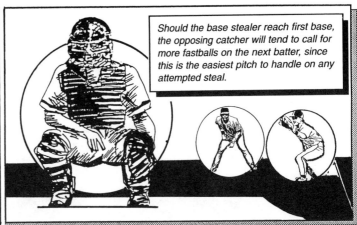

*Should the base stealer reach first base, the opposing catcher will tend to call for more fastballs on the next batter, since this is the easiest pitch to handle on any attempted steal.*

## Offense

*Two of the first-base coach's roles are to assist with his runner's lead and to alert him to a possible pickoff by the catcher.*

*By studying the first baseman's movements as the pitch is delivered to the plate, the first-base coach can tell if a pickoff is likely and alert his runner to get back to the bag.*

## Offense

When trying to advance from first to third on a base hit to right, the skilled base runner picks up instruction from the third-base coach about 20 feet before he touches second base. By learning his destination early, he can either round second without breaking stride or he can stop right on the bag should he be held up.

The same tactic is used when the runner tries to advance from second to home on a base hit.

85

## Offense

*Proper execution of the squeeze bunt requires both the batter and the runner at third base to remain still until just before the pitcher releases the ball. Any premature movements will cause the pitcher to alter his pitch or step off the rubber, nullifying the play.*

*Once the ball is released, the batter **must** bunt it and the runner breaks for home without turning back.*

## Offense

*In a sacrifice bunt situation, with runners on first and second, the batter should be wary of bunting down the third-base side against a left-handed pitcher.*

*While fielding the bunt on the third-base side, the left-handed pitcher, unlike the right-handed pitcher, does not need to pivot his body to throw to third base for the force-out. Therefore, he is quicker. The batter should bunt instead toward the first-base side.*

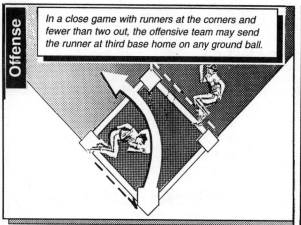

In a close game with runners at the corners and fewer than two out, the offensive team may send the runner at third base home on any ground ball.

This offensive maneuver is designed to entice the defense into making a play at home instead of turning a double play.

Should the runner be thrown out at home, the offense only gives up one out and still retains runners at first and second for the next batter.

## Offense

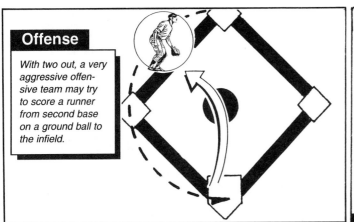

*With two out, a very aggressive offensive team may try to score a runner from second base on a ground ball to the infield.*

*The offense is counting on the runner's speed, a sloppy thrown from the infielder to first base rendering the batter safe, as well as the time it takes for the first baseman to recover from his stretch and throw to the plate.*

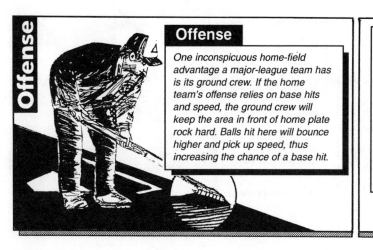

## Offense

*One inconspicuous home-field advantage a major-league team has is its ground crew. If the home team's offense relies on base hits and speed, the ground crew will keep the area in front of home plate rock hard. Balls hit here will bounce higher and pick up speed, thus increasing the chance of a base hit.*

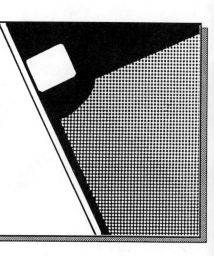

*Also, if the home team bunts well, prior to the season the ground crew will extend the turf right next to the base lines, thus maximizing the chance of bunted balls staying fair.*

Defensive strategies

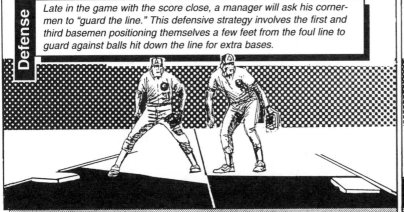

**Defense**

Late in the game with the score close, a manager will ask his cornermen to "guard the line." This defensive strategy involves the first and third basemen positioning themselves a few feet from the foul line to guard against balls hit down the line for extra bases.

Also, if a ball does get by to the cornerman's infield side, it is usually just a single, and the double play is in order for the next batter.

In a fine-tuned defense, the pitcher and the catcher are not the only players aware of the coming pitch selection.

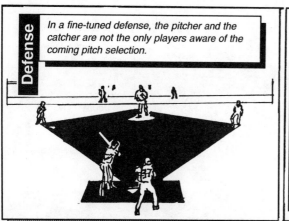

Along with the pitcher, the second baseman and shortstop check the catcher's signal and they, in turn, secretly relay the coming pitch to both the outfielders and cornermen. Now all nine defensive players can position themselves accordingly.

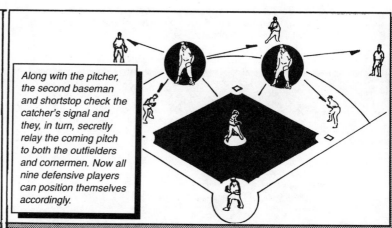

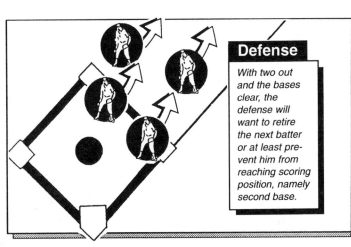

## Defense

With two out and the bases clear, the defense will want to retire the next batter or at least prevent him from reaching scoring position, namely second base.

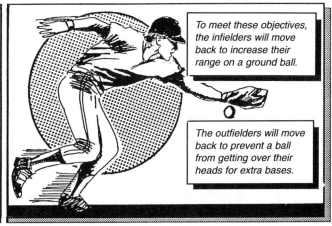

To meet these objectives, the infielders will move back to increase their range on a ground ball.

The outfielders will move back to prevent a ball from getting over their heads for extra bases.

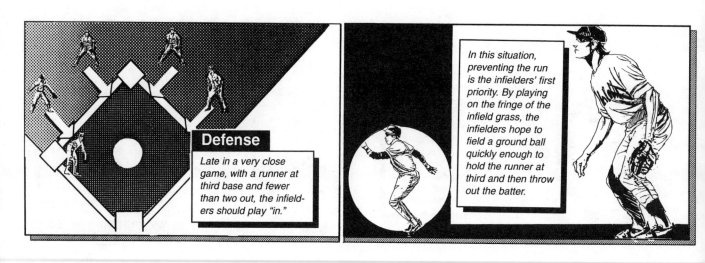

## Defense

Late in a very close game, with a runner at third base and fewer than two out, the infielders should play "in."

In this situation, preventing the run is the infielders' first priority. By playing on the fringe of the infield grass, the infielders hope to field a ground ball quickly enough to hold the runner at third and then throw out the batter.

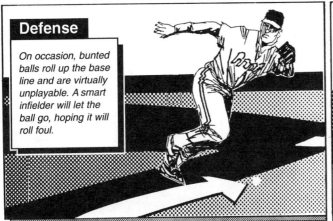

## Defense

*On occasion, bunted balls roll up the base line and are virtually unplayable. A smart infielder will let the ball go, hoping it will roll foul.*

*The same strategy is used by the outfielder in allowing a deep foul fly ball to drop when tagging runners are in scoring position and there is no chance of throwing them out.*

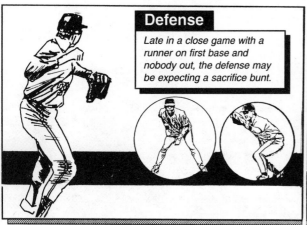

## Defense

*Late in a close game with a runner on first base and nobody out, the defense may be expecting a sacrifice bunt.*

*To uncover this suspected offense strategy, the pitcher will attempt to pick off the runner. This allows the catcher to watch the batter's top hand. If the top hand inches up the bat prematurely, then a bunt is likely on the next pitch.*

## Defense

In a rundown, the defense tries to stick to three rules. First, they try to push the runner back to the base he came from. Second, they try to retire the runner using fewer than two throws.

Finally, the defense tries to align itself on one side of the runner, to avoid criss-cross throwing.

## Defense

*The "daylight pickoff" is a pickoff attempt at second base between the pitcher and the shortstop. If the pitcher sees daylight between the advancing shortstop and the retreating base runner, he will turn and throw to second base.*

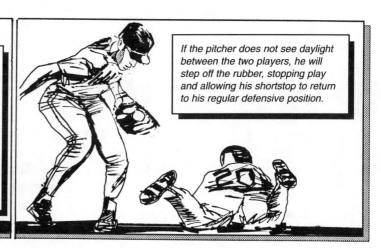

*If the pitcher does not see daylight between the two players, he will step off the rubber, stopping play and allowing his shortstop to return to his regular defensive position.*

## Defense

*A left-handed first baseman has three distinct advantages over a right-handed first baseman. First, on an attempted pickoff, the lefty need only catch the ball and apply the tag.*

*Second, since the glove is on his right hand, he has more range on balls hit to his right. Finally, he can start a double play faster because his throwing shoulder is already open toward second base.*

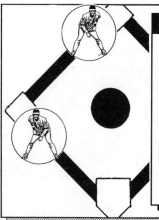

## Defense

*The lack of action surrounding an intentional walk often overshadows the defensive rationale behind it. With runners at second and third, the intentional walk creates a potential force-out at every base.*

*Second, with men on base and first base open, the intentional pass can nullify a dangerous hitter and allow the pitcher to pitch to a weaker hitter in the opposition's batting order.*

**Umpiring**

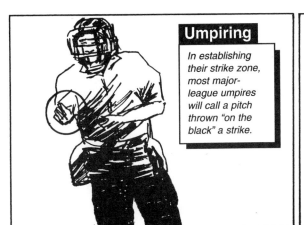

## Umpiring

In establishing their strike zone, most major-league umpires will call a pitch thrown "on the black" a strike.

The "black," although not technically part of the strike zone, is a one-inch border of dirt on either side of the 17-inch plate. Pitchers who can consistently "paint the black" are capitalizing on a wider, 19-inch strike zone.

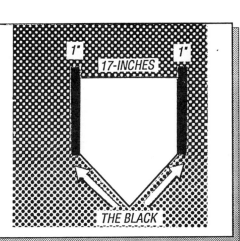

1"  17-INCHES  1"

THE BLACK

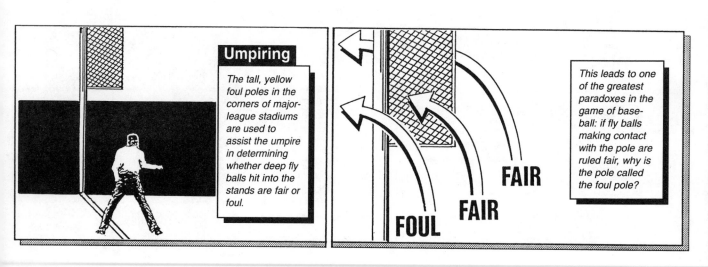

## Umpiring

The tall, yellow foul poles in the corners of major-league stadiums are used to assist the umpire in determining whether deep fly balls hit into the stands are fair or foul.

This leads to one of the greatest paradoxes in the game of baseball: if fly balls making contact with the pole are ruled fair, why is the pole called the foul pole?

FOUL  FAIR  FAIR

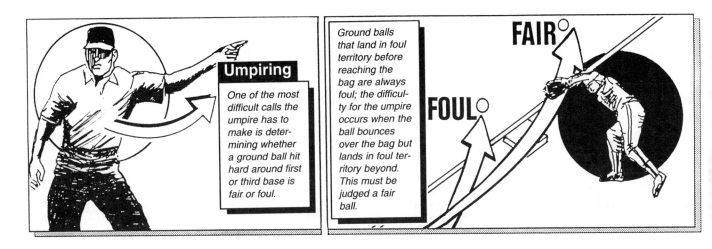

## Umpiring

One of the most difficult calls the umpire has to make is determining whether a ground ball hit hard around first or third base is fair or foul.

Ground balls that land in foul territory before reaching the bag are always foul; the difficulty for the umpire occurs when the ball bounces over the bag but lands in foul territory beyond. This must be judged a fair ball.

FAIR○

FOUL○

## Umpiring

A "banger," which is an umpire's word for a close play at first base, requires great concentration and quick decision in the heat of the game.

During the play, the umpire will watch for the runner's foot to touch the bag while listening for the ball to "smack" into the first base-man's mitt. His call will be based on which he hears or sees first.

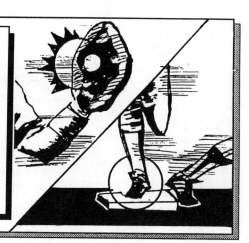

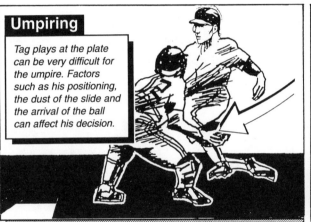

## Umpiring

*Tag plays at the plate can be very difficult for the umpire. Factors such as his positioning, the dust of the slide and the arrival of the ball can affect his decision.*

*If possible, the catcher will initiate contact and tag the runner about five feet up the line. In this way, the runner cannot reach the plate, so the umpire must call him out.*

109

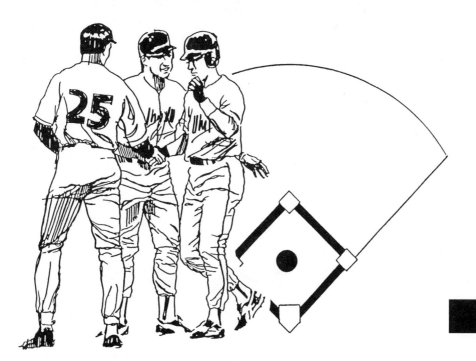

General

## General

Proper throwing mechanics are a must for catchers and fielders. In an effort to throw the ball accurately, they should grip the ball across the seams. Also, a proper arm slot requires the elbow and the shoulder to be parallel to the ground, forming a 90-degree angle with the upright forearm. Finally, they should try to release the ball by snapping straight down, not to the side, thus forming another 90-degree angle.

90° ANGLE

The cross-over step is a technique used by fielders to get to the ball faster and by base stealers to get a good jump on an attempted steal.

General

When players are moving to their left, they pivot their left foot and cross over their left leg with their right. This eliminates costly starter steps.

114

## General

*When an infielder has to turn 180 degrees to throw, he should pivot in the direction of his glove hand. This is the fastest way to open his throwing shoulder toward his target.*

*This same maneuver is used by an outfielder on balls hit over his head. By turning toward his glove side, he needs fewer steps to get into position to catch the ball.*

## General

In order to catch pop-ups or high fly balls in the sun, most major-leaguers will use flip-up sunglasses.

Only when the fielder determines the trajectory of the ball, usually at its apex, will he flip down his sunglasses to shield his eyes.

If he flips his sunglasses down just as the ball is hit, he could lose sight of the ball due to the sudden change in glare.

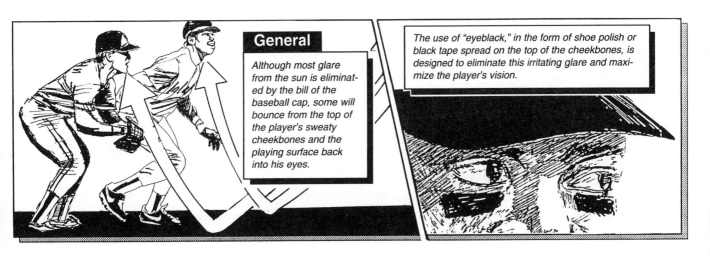

**General**

*Although most glare from the sun is eliminated by the bill of the baseball cap, some will bounce from the top of the player's sweaty cheekbones and the playing surface back into his eyes.*

*The use of "eyeblack," in the form of shoe polish or black tape spread on the top of the cheekbones, is designed to eliminate this irritating glare and maximize the player's vision.*

## General

Between pitches, with a runner on first base, some middle infielders can be seen facing each other while hiding their mouths behind their gloves.

They are communicating who will cover second base on an attempted steal. This must be kept secret from the offense as they may try to hit through the spot they suspect will be vacated by the middle infielder covering the bag.

## General

*During the pre-game warm-ups, players will study which side of second base the opposing middle infielders pivot toward when turning a double play.*

*Should a player find himself running toward second base on a ground ball, he must know where to slide in order to make contact with the infielder and break up the double play.*

## General

*During a pause in the action, base runners should pay attention to where the outfielders are positioned. Based on where the ball is hit, this information can help the runner decide whether to advance one or more bases, tag up or go half way.*

*Usually, balls hit to the left side of the outfielder will allow the base runner to take the extra base, since the outfielder is moving away from the base he needs to throw to.*

## General

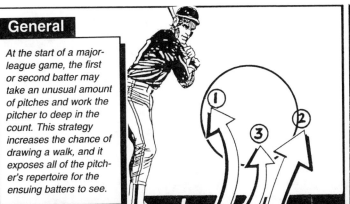

At the start of a major-league game, the first or second batter may take an unusual amount of pitches and work the pitcher to deep in the count. This strategy increases the chance of drawing a walk, and it exposes all of the pitcher's repertoire for the ensuing batters to see.

Also, if in later innings the pitcher gets two quick outs in two pitches, the third batter will usually take a few pitches to force the pitcher to work harder and to extend the inning.

## General

*Baseball is not without etiquette in all parts of the game, including autographing baseballs.*

*Major-league players always sign their names across the ball from one seam to the other. It is a faux pas to sign parallel to the seams. Also, the space where the seams are closest is reserved for each team's all-stars or team leaders.*

## General

Etiquette in baseball is not restricted to the field. Spectators often leave their seats for refreshments at the end of an inning.

Well-mannered spectators display the courtesy of waiting in the aisle until after an out before returning to their seats. They do not disturb others by returning during play.

# Notes

## Notes

**Notes**

# Notes

# Notes

live Better ashtanga yoga

# live Better ashtanga yoga

exercises and inspirations for well-being

## Anton Simmha

Thorsons
Directions for Life

**Live Better: Ashtanga Yoga**
by Anton Simmha

With love and respect to the memory of
Derek Ireland and the global Ashtanga family.

Thorsons
An imprint of HarperCollins*Publishers*
77–85 Fulham Palace Road
Hammersmith, London, England W6 8JB

Published in the United States by Thorsons
in 2003

Conceived, created, and designed by
Duncan Baird Publishers Ltd.
Sixth Floor
Castle House
75–76 Wells Street
London W1T 3QH

Managing Editor: Judy Barratt
Editor: Lucy Latchmore
Managing Designer: Manisha Patel
Designer: Allan Sommerville
Picture Research: Cecilia Weston-Baker
Commissioned Photography: Matthew Ward

Library of Congress Cataloging-in-Publication
Data is available.

10 9 8 7 6 5 4 3 2 1

ISBN: 0-00-766243-2

Typeset in Filosofia and Son Kern
Color reproduction by Scanhouse, Malaysia
Printed and bound by Imago, Thailand

PUBLISHER'S NOTE
Before following any advice or practice
suggested in this book, it is recommended
that you consult your doctor as to its
suitability, especially if you suffer from any
health problems or special conditions. The
publishers, author, and photographers
cannot accept any responsibility for any
injuries or damage incurred as a result of
following the exercises in this book, or of
using any of the therapeutic techniques
described or mentioned here.

# contents

# INTRODUCTION

My path toward Ashtanga yoga began during the late 1980s, while I was working in London as an artist and designer. At the time my main preoccupation was party-ing – something that I did with a passion bordering on the extreme. But after years of extreme living, I had pushed my body to the limits of physical endurance and abuse. I knew that I had to change my lifestyle radically, and so I began a search for balance and peace that was to be the beginning of my spiritual awakening.

At this point I had been practising yoga in London, on and off, for a couple of years. Then, while on holiday in Goa, South India, I was fortunate enough to meet an extraordinary man, called Derek Ireland, who introduced me to a form of yoga that I had never seen before – Ashtanga *Vinyasa* yoga!

Inspired by watching Derek perform this graceful practice on the beach, the "yoga penny" finally dropped. I suddenly knew that Ashtanga was the answer if I wanted to heal my body, my mind and my spirit.

The purpose of this book is to introduce you to the practice and concepts of Ashtanga *Vinyasa* yoga, in the hope that yoga may help you as it has helped me. It is intended as a beginner's introduction to the discipline and contains an abbreviated version of the Primary Series – the foundation sequence of Ashtanga yoga.

It is important to stress that this book should serve only as an aid to your practice, giving you some introductory insights into the purpose, techniques and benefits of this ancient system. It should not be used as a replacement for a qualified teacher.

Before attempting any of the exercises in this book, read the text all the way through to gain an overview of the subject. When you come to the exercises, read them through twice. The second time visualize yourself doing each step in turn to help you remember them better.

Above all, always follow this fundamental rule: never force, never stress, never strain, never overexert. Learn to listen to your body – it will always tell you how far to go.

Good luck. *Namaste* – Anton

Chapter One

# about ashtanga

Ashtanga *Vinyasa* yoga is a form of Hatha (physical) yoga that, like other physical forms, uses postures and breathing techniques as a starting point for attaining a state of "yoga" or "union". This is the ultimate goal of any type of yoga and involves the yoking together of mind, body and spirit so that we can experience self-realization or enlightenment.

Ashtanga yoga is unique in its use of *vinyasas* (breath-synchronized movements), which link the yoga postures together to form dynamic sequences. This book covers four sequences of postures, which together comprise a basic form of the Primary Series. This is the first of six Ashtanga series, the others

8

being the Intermediate Series and Advanced Series A, B, C and D. The Primary Series is sometimes called "Yoga Chikitsa", meaning "Yoga Therapy". This name refers to the healing nature of the series, which aims to create a strong, light, energetic body and a clear and focused mind in preparation for the more demanding postures of later series.

In this chapter we trace the history, aims and philosophy of Ashtanga yoga, the specific techniques that this form involves and the range of benefits these can bring you – whether you want to improve your fitness and flexibility or, on a deeper level, seek more spiritual meaning in your life.

# A BRIEF HISTORY OF ASHTANGA

Yoga is a living tradition, which emerged during the ancient Vedic civilization of India around 2800BCE. Throughout the centuries this tradition has been preserved by generations of teachers, who have passed on their wisdom verbally to their students. A number of these teachers have developed their own individual styles of yoga, resulting in the various different forms of the practice in existence today.

Ashtanga *Vinyasa* yoga is based on the teachings of a celebrated guru called Sri T Krishnamacharya and was popularized in the latter part of the twentieth century by its principal proponent and modern-day guru, Sri K Pattabhi Jois of Mysore, South India.

Pattabhi Jois (or Guruji as he is known by his students) began studying yoga under the tutelage of Sri T Krishnamacharya at the age of twelve in 1927. It is reputed that during the 1930s Krishnamacharya was carrying out research in the university library of Calcutta when he discovered an ancient Sanskrit manuscript

10

called the *Yoga Korunta*, written by an ancient seer called Vamana Rishi. The exact age of this document remains shrouded in mystery, but it is believed to be somewhere between two thousand and five thousand years old.

With the help of Guruji (also a Sanskrit scholar), Krishnamacharya translated the *Yoga Korunta* to reveal the outline of Ashtanga *Vinyasa* yoga – a form of yoga based on a detailed system of counting breaths into and out of postures, combined with ordered sequences of movement. Guruji has become the principal teacher of this form of yoga, and is the founder of the Ashtanga Yoga Research Institute, which conducts research into the health benefits of Ashtanga.

During the 1960s and 1970s, increasing numbers of Westerners travelled to India in search of alternative ways of life. A few of these individuals trained with Guruji in Mysore and were later responsible for introducing Ashtanga to the West. Since then this dynamic and physically challenging type of yoga has become popular in many countries around the world, as people look for holistic approaches to health and fitness.

# THE EIGHT LIMBS OF ASHTANGA

The word "Ashtanga" derives from the Sanskrit *ast*, meaning "eight", and *anga*, meaning "limbs". It refers to the systematic approach to life outlined in the *Yoga Sutras* – an important yogic text written by the sage Patanjali, between 200BCE and 200CE.

Patanjali envisioned the eight limbs of yoga as the interconnecting branches of a tree. *Asana* (posture practice) and *pranayama* (controlled breathing) are two of these limbs. The remaining six limbs are *yama* (ethics), *niyama* (self-discipline), *pratyahara* (withdrawal of the senses), *dharana* (concentration), *dhyana* (meditation) and *samadhi* (union with the true self). Working on any one limb encourages the others to grow in turn, leading ultimately toward enlightenment.

Ashtanga yoga focuses initially on *asana* and *pranayama* (covered in chapters two to five). As your practice develops you may wish to draw on the remaining six limbs (discussed in chapter six) in order to extend yoga into other areas of your life.

# SEEKING BALANCE

As children we exist "freely" — in a natural state of balance between mind and body in which thought and movement are seamless. As we grow into adulthood, most of us are conditioned to focus on the mind's capabilities at the expense of the body's and our natural state of balance is lost.

As we move and breathe in the practice of yoga, we reestablish the balance between mind and body. The ancient yogis explained this realignment with reference to what they called the three "Bodies of Man": the Physical Body (called Stula), the Astral or Subtle Body (Sukshma) and the Causal Body (Karana). Each of these bodies comprises one or more "sheaths", of which there are five in total. The Physical Body has only one sheath, the food sheath (known as the *annamaya kosha*). The Astral Body comprises three sheaths: the pranic or vital sheath (*pranamaya kosha*), the mental sheath (*manomaya kosha*) and the intellectual sheath (*vijnana-maya kosha*). The Causal Body has one sheath, called the blissful sheath (*anandamaya kosha*). The five sheaths fit together like the layers of a Russian doll, one inside the other, with the *annamaya kosha* the outermost and the *anandamaya kosha* the innermost.

Through the practice of Ashtanga yoga, we aim to bring into balance each of the bodies and their respective sheaths in order to reconnect with the *bindu*, the seed of the true self that lies at the centre of the *anandamaya kosha*. We do this initially by combining the controlled rhythm of *pranayama* breathing with the *vinyasa* movements of Ashtanga to encourage the body to relax, stretch and open. This helps us to move safely into the physical postures of yoga, which realign and strengthen our skeletal and muscular structures, stimulate and cleanse our internal organs and enhance the flow of energy throughout the body as a whole.

By focusing our attention entirely on the rhythm of the breath and the synchronized movements of the body, we learn to still the mind, centring it within the body. In so doing, the mind and the body become one as we move toward the state of "yoga" or "union".

# THE BODY'S ENERGY SYSTEM

Ancient yogis described the structure of the vital sheath (*pranamaya kosha*) as a network of interconnecting energy channels called the "subtle anatomy" – a system similar to the meridian networks of Chinese medicine. In the yogic tradition these channels are called *nadis* and distribute *prana* (vital life force) throughout the body.

It is believed that there are 72,000 *nadis*. The most important is the *sushumna nadi*, a central pranic tube that runs the length of the spinal column, from the perineum, below the groin, up to the crown of the head. Two other major *nadis* – the *ida* and *pingala* – crisscross the *sushumna nadi* and connect to the left and right nostrils respectively. These channels intersect with the *sushumna nadi* at seven key points called *chakras*. The *chakras* are the main energy centres of the body and their positions correspond to the various nerve plexuses of the spinal cord (see illustration, p.19). The *chakras* distribute energy throughout the subtle anatomy and can be envisaged as spinning spheres of light.

The breathing techniques and postures of yoga help to balance the flow of *prana* through the vital sheath. When we inhale in a controlled fashion through our nostrils, *prana* enters the *ida* and *pingala nadis*, where it is distributed throughout the energetic system. Performing the postures stimulates the movement of the *prana* through the *nadis* and *chakras*, clearing the blockages that often result from the stresses of Western living.

### The Chakras

- The red *muladhara* or root *chakra* is located by the perineum, at the base of the spine. It symbolizes our primal connection to the earth element. Focusing upon it grounds us, giving a sense of security and belonging.

- The orange *swadhisthana* or sacral *chakra* is located just above the genitals and symbolizes our place of origin. Its energy governs sexuality and creativity, and it corresponds to the water element.

- The yellow *manipura* or solar plexus *chakra* lies behind the navel, at our centre. It connects us with the energy of the sun and provides us with the impetus for all our actions – it is the source of our willpower. It also correlates to the fire element: by focusing on the *manipura chakra* we can stoke our *agni* or "internal fire".

- The green *anahata* (heart) *chakra* is situated close to the heart organ in the central chest area. This is the emotional centre of the body – the seat of compassion and unconditional love – and relates to the air element.

- The blue throat *chakra* is called *vishuddha*, meaning purity. Located at the base of the neck, it is the centre of expression and knowledge and is governed by ether.

- The purple "third eye" *chakra* is called *ajna*, meaning "inner eye", and is located in the middle of the forehead, just above the eyebrows. It is the centre for spiritual vision, ruling our intellectual thought processes and connecting us to the wisdom of the cosmos.

- The crown *chakra* on top of the head is called *sahasrara*, which means "a thousand petals". It is depicted as a full-blossomed lotus flower and is believed to radiate a thousand rays of light from its centre. This *chakra* connects us to the universal consciousness, and meditating on it moves us toward a realization of our true selves.

sahasrara

ajna

vishuddha

anahata

manipura

swadhisthana

muladhara

# THE VINYASA SYSTEM

It is the *vinyasa* system that makes Ashtanga *Vinyasa* yoga unique. The term *vinyasa* refers to the breath-synchronized movements that link the various yoga postures together, creating a "dynamic flow" throughout the practice. This fluidity of movement and breathing differentiates Ashtanga from other forms of Hatha yoga, in which rests are often taken between postures.

One of the main functions of the *vinyasa* system is to generate an intense heat called *agni* within the internal organs that will then permeate throughout the rest of the body. The benefits of this heat are twofold: first, it is deeply purifying, encouraging the body to release toxins as sweat through the skin; second, it encourages the body to become more malleable, like heated metal, enabling it to stretch with minimum risk of injury.

**The Vinyasa Movement**

The *vinyasa* movement is in fact a sequence of movements. The *vinyasa* itself is based on sun salutation A (see pp.38–41), a sequence of movements that is often performed several times at the start of a yoga session. In addition to heating the body, practising these movements helps us to develop strength and stamina throughout the upper torso as well as realigning the skeletal and muscular structures of the body after each posture. Beginners can find the *vinyasa* movement rather challenging at first, so I have omitted the *vinyasas* between the standing postures (with the exception of the warrior sequence; see pp.66-71) and have included a modified version of the half-*vinyasa* (see pp.76–7), to be practised after each sitting posture (or after each side of each sitting posture when you feel ready).

## The Vinyasa Breath

The breathing technique used synchronistically within both the *vinyasa* movements and the postures that they link is called *ujjayi*, which means "victorious". The aim is to sustain this form of breathing throughout the course of the yoga practice, synchronizing every movement with either an inhalation or an exhalation. In each case the impulse to move originates with the breath. The exercises in chapters two to five explain how the various movements fit together with the breathing.

When we practise *ujjayi* breathing, we create a unique sound in the back of the throat that is reminiscent of the rush of distant waves. We can create this sound by breathing through the nostrils, softening the palate and narrowing the epiglottis (the aperture at the back of the throat). This narrowing catches the breath momentarily, enabling us to control the breath as it flows into and out of our lungs. We are aiming to keep each in-breath and out-breath identical in terms of both duration and effort. When this is achieved the breathing cycle becomes more circular as the natural pauses between breaths diminish, creating a rolling breath that leaves no real distinction between inhalations and exhalations.

To experience your own *ujjayi* sound, sit in a comfortable and relaxed position, place your hands over your ears and breathe in and out, sighing audibly with your mouth open. This will produce an "ahh" and a "haa" sound. Once you can do this successfully, close your mouth and breathe through your nose, but continue to make the "ahh" and "haa" sounds by maintaining the slight constriction at the back of your throat. Breathe within your normal capacity – you are trying to create an even and relaxed breath, so do not puff up your chest or force the exhalation. Allow your entire ribcage to open as you breathe into the front, sides and back of your upper chest, expanding your lungs fully. As you do so try to keep your abdomen soft and still, lightly drawn in and up without locking it tight. This will create a bridge of support for your internal organs during your practice.

When you first begin practising Ashtanga yoga, you will probably find that most of your attention is occupied with following the sequence of movements for each exercise. However, when these become more familiar you will be able to direct more of your attention to synchronizing your movements with the breath. Try to focus on the rushing sound of the *ujjayi* breath, treating it like a mantra. This will transform your practice into a moving meditation that quietens your thoughts and emotions, enhancing your internal awareness.

# THE BANDHAS

As you become more familiar with the movements and breathing of the *vinyasa* system, try to incorporate the *bandhas* into your yoga practice. *Bandha* is a Sanskrit word meaning "to lock, catch or seal". In terms of Ashtanga yoga, the *bandhas* are internal locks created by the gentle contraction of muscles within specific areas of the body. These function rather like valves, working together to contain and direct *prana* upward through the *nadis* of the subtle anatomy. Holding these locks provides the extra energy necessary for sustaining the momentum of an Ashtanga practice and helps to contain the heat generated by the *vinyasas*. In physical terms *bandhas* support the lower back and internal organs as well as aiding *ujjayi* breathing.

There are three *bandhas* used in Ashtanga: *mula bandha* or root lock, *uddiyana bandha* or lower abdominal lock and *jalandhara bandha*, throat lock. *Mula bandha* is achieved at the base of the spine and is responsible for retaining *prana* within the body. You can locate it by drawing up the muscles of the anal sphincter at the end of an exhalation. As you become more sensitive in this area, you will find that your awareness shifts slightly forward to your perineum, just below the genitals.

*Uddiyana bandha* is achieved in the lower abdominal region. When held it encourages *prana* to flow upward through the *nadis* of the subtle anatomy. To locate this lock draw your abdomen in and up at the end of an exhalation, when your lungs are empty. Continue to hold your abdomen in this position as you inhale – you are aiming for a soft stillness (not a hard crunching) in your lower belly that you can sustain during your practice.

*Jalandhara bandha* is a throat lock that is engaged when practising certain *pranayama* techniques. You should practise it only under qualified supervision.

Initially it is difficult to grasp the subtlety of the *bandhas* without the help of a teacher, but with practice you will find them easier to locate and sustain during your yoga sessions. When you do you will find that they transform your practice, giving you an internal strength and lightness that enhances every movement.

# THE DRISHTIS

In each of the exercises in the book, you will find that as you hold each posture you are instructed to look toward certain points on your body or in your surroundings. These gaze points are called *drishtis*. Focusing on these points during your practice will prevent your eyes from wandering around your surroundings. This helps the mind to concentrate and to develop a deeper internal focus on the body – on the action of the *ujjayi* breath, the physical movements of the postures, the muscular contractions of the *bandhas* and any other sensations that arise during your practice.

Ashtanga yoga uses nine *drishtis*, which you will find referred to in each of the exercises. These are as follows: the tip of the nose (*nasagrai*); the thumbs (*angusta ma dyai*); the "third eye" (*broomadhya*), located in the middle of the forehead, just above the eyebrows; the navel (*nabi*); up to the sky (*urdhva*); the hand (*hastagrai*); the toes (*padhayoragrai*); the far left (*parsva*); and the far right (*parsva*).

# ATTITUDES TO YOUR PRACTICE

If yoga is to benefit you, it is important to cultivate healthy attitudes toward your practice. Ashtanga is a physically challenging form of yoga, so it is important to develop sensitivity toward your body. Such awareness will ensure the safety of your practice, helping you to find and maintain correct postural alignment and to avoid overstraining your muscles.

Before embarking upon a yoga session, take a few moments to tune into your body, checking for any areas of pain or tension. Where these exist you may need to adapt your practice accordingly, avoiding any postures that could aggravate your condition. While one of the reasons for practising yoga is to challenge ourselves, we should do so without causing pain or injury. To do this we must be aware of our limits within each posture. When easing yourself into a posture, you will discover what are known as your "minimum edge" and "maximum edge". Your minimum edge is the point at which you first feel a stretch in a posture. Your maximum edge is your "surrender point" – the furthest you can stretch before you come up against your body's natural wall of resistance. If you force your body to stretch beyond this point, you may experience pain or discomfort and risk injuring yourself. Instead try to relax into the position by focusing on your breathing. This is called "dying to the pose" or "surrendering to the breath", and it allows your body to expand its natural limits at its own pace, without causing any damage.

By letting the wisdom of your body take charge of your practice, you move beyond the desires and expectations of your ego, which seeks to push your body beyond its limits for the sake of immediate achievement. It is more beneficial to focus on the state of your body in the present, allowing it to relax and open of its own accord.

This attitude of patience is also essential when dealing with the mind. During your practice you may notice your attention wandering. Try not to become frustrated with yourself. Instead simply return your focus to your breathing. This will quieten the mind's activity, returning you to the present moment in your body.

# KEY POINTS FOR PRACTICE

1  Wait at least two hours after a heavy meal before practising yoga, and in the first hour after your session eat only lightly. During your practice keep drinking to a minimum, taking only a few sips of water if you need to.

2  If possible allocate a set time each day in which to practise yoga. The ideal time is first thing in the morning, but if this is not possible simply choose the time that is most convenient for you.

3  Try to practise regularly. Remember that little and often is better than sessions that are longer but infrequent.

4  Practise yoga in a well-heated room. This will ensure that you maintain enough internal body heat to prevent your muscles from becoming cold, thereby reducing the risk of injury.

5  Create a soothing environment to help you to relax. Try lighting some candles or burning some incense.

6  Try to minimize distractions during your yoga session. Choose a quiet room in which to practise and switch off your television, radio, telephone and mobile phone.

7   Wear light, loose, comfortable clothing and remove your shoes and socks, your watch and any jewelry.

8   Buy a yoga mat. This will provide you with a safe, nonslip surface on which to work.

9   When trying Ashtanga yoga for the first time, build up your practice slowly. Begin by doing the sun salutations from the Warm-up Sequence, followed by the cool-down poses from the Finishing Sequence. Gradually incorporate the standing postures and the floor postures as you feel your strength and stamina increasing.

10   Use your breath as a guide. If your breathing has quickened, you are probably trying too hard. Pause and relax for a moment. Reestablish an even rhythm in your breathing before continuing with your practice.

11   If you feel faint or light-headed, stop and rest.

12   Look for a yoga class or teacher in your area. This will be invaluable for developing your practice further.

13   If you are pregnant, feel unwell or have a medical condition, seek the advice of your doctor before beginning an unsupervised yoga practice.

14   Have fun!

... Our yesterdays are but dreams

Our tomorrows merely visions

But today lived well makes

Every yesterday a dream of joy,

And each tomorrow a vision of promise ...

ATTRIBUTED TO KALIDASA

SANSKRIT POEM "THE SALUTATION OF THE DAWN" (5TH CENTURY CE)

Chapter Two

# the warm-up sequence

The Warm-up Sequence is composed of two sets of
movements called sun salutation A and sun salutation
B. These are repeated several times at the beginning
of a practice and in modifed forms later on. The
sun salutations comprise a series of movements
synchronized with *ujjayi* breathing and, as such, form
the basis for the *vinyasa* (see pp.20–23). Performed at
the beginning of an Ashtanga practice, they serve to
generate *agni*, or internal heat, within our bodies.
This heat increases our flexibility, allowing us to open
up our bodies safely and effectively during the
posture sequences without straining muscles or
damaging ligaments and tendons.

34

The Warm-up Sequence is the foundation stone of the Ashtanga practice. It is also the perfect training ground for beginners, teaching us how to connect up the breath and the movements of the *vinyasa* system. The first few times that you practise the Warm-up Sequence, concentrate on mastering sun salutation A, before attempting the more complex sun salutation B. To begin with, repeat the sun salutations three times each, increasing the number of repetitions to five as your fitness, strength and flexibility improves.

Try practising sun salutations in the mornings before breakfast — they will increase your energy levels and concentration for the rest of the day.

The Lord of Love lies beyond and yet within us.
He is unborn, without body and mind, name or form.
Yet he is the source of all:
Space, air, fire, water and earth –
The elements from which life is created.

MUNDAKA UPANISHAD (5TH CENTURY BCE)

# SUN SALUTATION A
## Surya Namaskara A

Adopt standing ready pose (*samasthiti*) with your feet together, arms by your sides and shoulders relaxed. Begin even and relaxed *ujjayi* breathing.

1 Inhaling, take your arms out to the side and bring them up above your head with your palms together. Look up at your thumbs.

standing ready pose       1       2

2  Exhaling, fold forward from your hips, taking your head toward your shins and placing your hands on the floor on either side of your feet (or on your ankles or shins).

3  Inhaling, extend your spine and look up, straightening your arms but keeping your fingertips on the floor.

4  Exhaling, bend your knees and transfer your weight into your hands as you jump or step back (keeping your arms straight) into a raised press-up position. (Your legs should be straight and your shoulders should be above your wrists.) Continuing the movement bend your arms, lowering your body until your chin almost touches the floor. Keep your elbows pressed into your sides and look ahead.

*(continued)*

3                          4

5   Inhaling, roll over your toes so that the tops of your feet are on the floor. Straighten your arms, bringing your chest through your hands. Keep your shoulders down and lift your chest. Raise your head and look up.

6   Exhaling, push back with your arms, roll back over your toes and lift your hips upward as you move into "downward dog" posture. Your hands should be shoulder-width apart, middle finger pointing forward, and your feet should be hip-width apart. Lengthen your spine and press down gently through your heels. Tuck in your chin and gaze toward your groin or navel. Hold this position for five full breaths (five inhalations and exhalations).

5                    6

7  Inhaling, jump or walk your feet toward your hands. Keep your fingertips on the floor as you extend your spine and look up.

8  Exhaling, fold forward from your hips, taking your head toward your shins and releasing your spine.

9  Inhaling, raise your torso and arms, bringing your palms together above your head. Look up at your thumbs. Exhale, lowering your arms to your sides. Repeat the whole sequence five times.

7                    8                    9

# SUN SALUTATION B
## Surya Namaskara B

1  Begin in standing ready pose. Inhaling, bend your knees and raise your arms above your head, bringing your palms together and looking up at your thumbs.

2  Exhaling, straighten your legs and fold forward from your hips, taking your head toward your shins and placing your hands on the floor on either side of your feet (or on your ankles or shins if necessary).

1                    2                    3

3  Inhaling, extend your spine as you look up, straightening your arms but keeping your hands down.

4  Exhaling, jump or step back into a raised press-up
position. Then, bending your arms, lower your body
until your chin almost touches the floor and look ahead.

5  Inhaling, roll over your toes and straighten your arms,
bringing your chest through your hands. Keep your
shoulders down, lift your chest and look up.

6  Exhaling, push back with your arms, roll back over your
toes on to the soles of your feet and lift your hips toward
the sky as you move into downward dog.

*(continued)*

4                    5                    6

7 Inhaling, turn your left foot out 45° and step your right foot between your hands. Continuing the inhalation, raise your torso, lifting your arms above your head and bringing your palms together. Look up at your thumbs.

8 Exhaling, lower your hands to the floor and step your right foot back alongside your left, bringing you into a raised press-up position. Bending your arms, gently lower your body until your chin almost touches the floor and look ahead.

7                    8

9   Inhaling, roll over your toes on to the tops of your feet
    and straighten your arms, bringing your chest through
    your hands. Keep your shoulders down, lift your chest
    and look up.

10  Exhaling, push back with your arms, roll back over your
    toes on to the soles of your feet and lift your hips toward
    the sky as you move into downward dog.

11  Inhaling, turn your right foot out 45°and step your left
    foot between your hands. Continuing the inhalation,
    raise your torso, lifting your hands above your head and
    bringing your palms together. Look up at your thumbs.

    *(continued)*

9                    10                    11

12   Exhaling, lower your hands to the floor and step your left foot back alongside your right, bringing you into a raised press-up position. Bending your arms, lower your body until your chin almost touches the floor and look ahead.

13   Inhaling, roll over your toes and straighten your arms, bringing your chest through your hands. Keep your shoulders down, lift your chest and look up.

14   Exhaling, push back with your arms, roll back over your toes and lift your hips toward the sky as you move into downward dog. Lengthen your spine and press down through your heels. Tuck in your chin and gaze toward your groin or navel. Hold for five full breaths.

12                    13                    14

15  Inhaling, jump or walk your feet toward your hands, keeping your hands down as you extend your spine and look up.

16  Exhaling, fold forward from your hips, taking your head toward your shins and releasing your spine.

17  Inhaling, bend your knees before raising your torso and arms, bringing your palms together above your head. Look up at your thumbs. Exhaling, return to standing ready pose. Repeat the whole sequence five times.

15                    16                    17

Body and breath, essence and energy are one:
when the body does not move, essence cannot flow;
when essence cannot flow, energy stagnates.

SUN SSU-MO, TANG-DYNASTY TAOIST PHYSICIAN

(581—681CE)

All living creatures depend on the breath
For it is the sustaining force of life itself,
Which determines how long all may live.
Those who revere breath as a gift from the Lord
Shall live to complete their full span of life.

TAITTIRIYA UPANISHAD (7TH CENTURY BCE)

# Chapter Three

# the standing sequence

Once you have completed the sun salutations, your body should feel warm and you may even have begun to sweat. This is the ideal state for embarking upon the standing postures, which continue the process of opening up the body, loosening the joints and stretching out the muscles on a deeper level.

The standing postures encourage the development of strength and balance throughout the body. When practising these postures pay particular attention to your feet, for these are your foundation, your points of contact with the earth. Work on spreading the soles of your feet and splaying your toes to enlarge your base – this will improve your balance and the strength of your postures. If you find yourself off-balance, check the alignment of your feet and, if necessary, adjust your position accordingly.

Each of the postures in the Standing Sequence begins with *samasthiti*, the standing ready pose (see p.38). As you progress through the postures for the first time, focus initially on learning the positions and the movements leading into and out of each posture. When the sequence becomes more familiar, you can begin to link these movements with your *ujjayi* breathing, remembering that the breath should always lead the movement. The *bandhas* and *drishtis* will come with time, so try to be patient with yourself.

# STANDING FORWARD BEND
## Padangusthasana

1   Begin in standing ready pose. Inhaling, jump or step
    your feet hip-width apart. Exhaling, place your hands on
    your hips and relax your shoulders.

2   Inhaling, look up, lift and open your chest, lengthen the
    front of your body and draw your abdomen in. Exhaling,
    fold forward from your hips, lower your arms and hook
    around your big toes with the first two fingers of each
    hand. (Hold your ankles or shins if you cannot reach
    your toes.) Inhaling, pull against your grip and look up,
    extending your spine fully.

3   Exhaling, draw yourself down toward your legs, bending
    your elbows out to the sides. Look toward the tip of your
    nose and hold the position for five full breaths. To
    finish, inhaling, return to position 1. Exhaling, jump or
    step your feet back to the standing ready pose.

    *This posture stretches the spine and backs of the legs; massages
    the liver, spleen and kidneys; and reduces abdominal fat.*

# STANDING FORWARD BEND

1    2    3

# EXTENDED TRIANGLE
## Utthita Trikonasana

1  Begin in standing ready pose. Inhaling, step to the right.
   Extend your arms horizontally out to the sides, palms
   down, and ensure that your feet line up beneath your
   elbows. Exhaling, turn your right foot out 90° and your
   left foot in 45°.

2  Inhaling, open your chest and lengthen your neck.
   Exhaling, fold sideways into your right hip, reaching
   down through your right arm to hook around your right
   big toe with your first two fingers. Extend up through
   your left arm, opening across your chest and shoulders.
   Turn your head to look up at your left thumb. Hold this
   position for five full breaths. Inhaling, return to position 1 and repeat the movement on your left side. To finish, inhaling, come up from the posture with your arms
   outstretched. Exhaling, return to standing ready pose.

*This posture strengthens and tones the legs, hips and back as
well as improving digestion and relieving breathing problems.*

# EXTENDED TRIANGLE

1

2

55

# EXTENDED SIDE ANGLE
## Utthita Parsvakonasana

1   Begin in standing ready pose. Inhaling, take a wide step
    to the right. Extend your arms horizontally out to the
    sides, palms down, and line up your feet beneath your
    wrists. Exhaling, turn your right foot out 90° and your
    left foot in 45°.

2   Inhaling, open your chest and shoulders. Exhaling,
    bend your right knee to form a right angle between your
    thigh and calf. Place your right hand outside your right
    foot, pressing your palm into the floor and your right
    knee into your armpit. Extend your left arm over your
    head and stretch down through your left foot. Look up at
    the extended hand and hold for five full breaths.
    Inhaling, return to position 1 and repeat the movement
    on your left side. To finish, inhaling, come up from the
    posture. Exhaling, return to standing ready pose.

*This posture opens the ribcage, strengthens the arms, upper
back, legs and hips, and improves digestion and breathing.*

1

2

# FEET SPREAD INSIDE STRETCH
## Prasarita Padottanasana

1    Begin in standing ready pose. Inhaling, take a wide step to the right. Extend your arms horizontally out to the sides and line up your feet beneath your wrists, with your heels in line and the outsides of your feet parallel.

2    Exhaling, lower your hands to your hips.

3    Inhaling, open your chest and look up. Exhaling, fold forward and place your hands on the floor, shoulder-width apart, with your elbows tucked in. Inhaling, straighten your arms, extend the spine and look up.

4    Exhaling, lower your torso, taking your head toward the floor and allowing your arms to bend. Look toward the tip of your nose and hold for five full breaths. To finish, inhaling, straighten your arms and look up. Exhaling, place your hands on your hips. Inhaling, come up to position 2. Exhaling, return to standing ready pose.

*This posture lengthens the inner thighs, stimulates the pelvic organs and encourages the flow of blood to the brain.*

1

2

3

4

# SIDE FORWARD STRETCH
## Parsvottanasana

1   Begin in standing ready pose. Inhaling, step to the right.
    Extend your arms horizontally to the sides, palms down,
    and line up your feet roughly beneath your elbows.
    Exhaling, turn your right foot out 90° and your left foot
    in 45°. Turning to face your right foot, bring your hips
    square and join your hands behind your back in prayer
    position. Inhaling, press your palms together, arch your
    spine, open your chest and look up.

2   Exhaling, fold forward toward your right shin, leading
    with your chin. (If necessary bend your right knee
    slightly.) Look toward your right big toe and hold this
    position for five full breaths. Inhaling, return to pos-
    ition 1 and repeat the movement on your left side. To
    finish come up on the sixth inhalation and bring your
    feet parallel. Exhaling, return to standing ready pose.

*This posture opens the hips, improves balance, tones the
abdomen and clears the digestive and respiratory tracts.*

1

2

# EXTENDED STANDING LEG RAISES
## Utthita Hasta Padangusthasana

1    Begin in standing ready pose. Inhaling, bend and raise your right leg, hooking around your big toe with the first two fingers of your right hand. Place your left hand on your left hip and grip firmly.

2    Exhaling, extend your right leg out as straight as possible in front of you, while maintaining your grip on your big toe. Look at the held toe or focus on a fixed point straight ahead of you to help you maintain your balance. Hold this position for five full breaths.

3    Inhaling, lift and open your chest. Exhaling, take your right leg out to the right. Turn your head to look over your left shoulder and focus on a fixed point. Hold the posture for five full breaths. Inhaling, return to position 2. Exhaling, release your grip and return to standing ready pose. Repeat the exercise with your left leg.

*This posture increases the flexibility of the hips, strengthens the legs and stimulates the kidneys and digestive system.*

1

2

3

# TREE POSE
## Vrkshasana

1   Begin in standing ready pose. Inhaling, shift your
    weight on to your left leg. Keeping your left leg straight,
    lift your right leg, taking hold of your right ankle with
    your right hand. Exhaling, place the sole of your right
    foot on the inside of your left thigh, bringing the heel as
    close to your groin as possible. Press the thigh and foot
    together while drawing your right knee back. Focus
    ahead on a fixed point to maintain balance.

2   Inhaling, lift your chest, roll your shoulders back and
    extend upward through your spine. Exhaling, bring your
    hands into prayer position in front of your chest. Look at
    the tip of your nose or focus on a fixed point ahead. Hold
    this position for five full breaths. Inhaling, lift the foot
    off the thigh. Exhaling, return to standing ready pose.
    Repeat the exercise on the left side.

*This posture strengthens the feet and ankles, opens the hips,
increases knee flexibility and improves balance and focus.*

1

2

## WARRIOR SEQUENCE
### Virabhadrasana

*The warrior sequence marks the end of the standing postures and provides a smooth transition into the floor postures. The sequence improves overall strength, flexibility and stamina, realigns the spine, opens the ribcage, stretches the inner thighs and tones the buttocks and abdominals.*

1   Starting from standing ready pose, perform steps 1–6 of sun salutation A (see pp.38–41). Hold position 6 (downward dog) for one full breath.

2    Inhaling, bend your knees and jump your feet toward your hands. Keeping your feet together and your knees bent, tuck in your tailbone as you sit down into the posture. Raise your arms, bringing your palms together above your head. Look up toward your thumbs and hold this position for five full breaths.

*(continued)*

2

3    Inhaling, straighten your legs, reaching up with your hands as you return to position 1 of sun salutation A. Move through steps 1–6 of sun salutation A, remaining in position 6 (downward dog) for one full breath.

4    Inhaling, turn your left foot out 45° and step your right foot toward your hands. Continuing the inhalation, bend your right knee to form a right angle between your thigh and calf, adjusting your feet if necessary. As you do so raise your torso, bringing your palms together above your head. Ensure that your back leg is straight and your back foot is flat on the floor. Look up at your thumbs. Hold the position for five full breaths.

3

5  Inhaling, keep your arms above your head with the palms pressed together as you straighten your right leg, pivot your left foot out and your right foot in, and rotate your body around to face the opposite direction. Exhaling, bend your left knee to form a right angle between your thigh and calf. Adjust the space between your feet if necessary and ensure that your back leg is straight and your back foot is flat on the floor. Look up at your thumbs. Hold the position for five full breaths.

*(continued)*

4                                    5

6   Exhaling, lower your arms until they extend out hori-
    zontally over your legs, palms down. Stretch out through
    your fingers, opening your chest and shoulders. Look
    toward the middle finger of your left hand. Hold the
    position for five full breaths.

7   Inhaling, keep your arms parallel to the floor as you
    straighten your left leg, pivoting your right foot out and
    your left foot in. As you do so rotate your body round to
    face the opposite direction. Exhaling, bend your right
    knee to form a right angle between your thigh and calf.

6                                          7

Adjust the space between your feet if necessary and ensure that your back leg is straight and your back foot is flat on the floor. Look toward the middle finger of your right hand. Hold the position for five full breaths.

8 Inhaling, move your left arm round so that it is next to your right. Exhaling, take your hands to the floor, on either side of your right foot, and step back into a raised press-up position. Lower yourself into position 4 of sun salutation A. Repeat steps 4–9 of sun salutation A, holding position 6 (downward dog) for one full breath.

8

Away from the chatter of the senses
From the restless wanderings of the mind
There is a quiet pool of stillness.
The wise call this stillness the highest state of being.
It is the place where we find unity.

Never to become separate again.

KATHA UPANISHAD (5TH CENTURY BCE)

It has its roots in the worlds above
And its branches on earth below.
It is the Tree of all Eternity.
Its pure root is Brahman – the Immortal Giver of Life
Whom none can transcend.

KATHA UPANISHAD (5TH CENTURY BCE)

# Chapter Four

# the floor sequence

The floor postures of the Primary Series extend the process that is begun in the Standing Sequence. We explore a new relationship with our foundation as our principal points of contact with the floor shift from our feet to our buttocks and hands, which provide a broader base and a lower centre of gravity. The result is a greater sense of stability that allows us to deepen our focus on the breath and enhance our internal awareness. The floor postures also bring us into greater contact with the root *chakra* (see pp.16–19), which has a grounding effect on our emotions.

A number of the postures in this chapter are forward bends, where the torso bends over the legs.

These serve to lengthen the spine, improving flexibility and opening the vertebrae, as well as stretching and lengthening the hamstrings. To counterbalance these postures the sequence also includes more open poses that flex the spine in the opposite direction.

A half-*vinyasa* (see pp.76–7) is performed between each posture: this chapter presents a modified version that is suitable for beginners. As well as linking the postures, half-*vinyasas* sustain the internal heat generated during the earlier sequences. They also rebalance and centre our bodies between postures, and work on our upper body and abdominal strength – helping us to develop greater internal support.

## HALF-VINYASA

1  Begin in sitting ready pose with your legs straight out in front of you, feet together, hands flat on the floor just behind your hips. Inhaling, cross your legs, bringing your feet as close to your buttocks as possible. Place your palms on the floor ahead of your feet, slightly more than shoulder-width apart with the fingers pointing forward.

2  Pressing down through your hands, roll forward over your ankles, lifting your buttocks off the floor.

3  Maintaining the lift during the exhalation, shift your weight forward and jump your legs backward into a raised press-up position. Bending your arms, lower your body until your chin almost touches the floor.

4  Inhaling, roll over your toes, straighten your arms, bring your chest through your arms and look up.

5  Exhaling, push back with your arms into downward dog. Hold this position for one full breath. Inhaling, return to position 2 by jumping your feet toward your hands, crossing your ankles as you land. Exhaling, straighten your legs in preparation for the next floor posture.

1

2

3

4

5

# STAFF POSTURE/SEATED FORWARD BEND
## Dandasana/Paschimattanasana

1 Adopt sitting ready pose with your legs straight out in front of you, feet together, and your hands flat on the floor, just behind your hips, fingers pointing forward. Inhaling, lift your chest and draw your shoulders back. Exhaling, lower your chin and flex your ankles. Look at your toes or your nose. Hold for five full breaths.

2 Inhaling, lift your chin, extend up through your spine and draw in your abdomen. Exhaling, reach forward and hook around your two big toes with the first two fingers of each hand. Inhaling, lengthen your spine and look up.

3 Exhaling, use your arms to draw yourself forward over your legs. Bend your elbows out to the sides as you extend your chin toward your shins. Look at your toes and hold for five full breaths. Inhaling, return to position 1. After exhaling perform a half-*vinyasa*.

*This posture stretches the spine and hamstrings, massages the internal organs and strengthens the heart.*

1

2

3

# INCLINED BACK LIFT
## Purvattanasana

1  Begin in sitting ready pose, pressing your palms into the floor and lifting your chest as you inhale. Exhaling, place your hands between 20 and 30 cm (7.9–11.8 in) behind your hips, shoulder-width apart with the fingers pointing forward.

2  Inhaling, raise your hips, keeping the legs and feet together. Gently allow your head to relax backward, without shortening your neck. Push the soles of your feet into the floor to help keep your legs straight and lift your pelvis. Push down through your hands, rolling your shoulders back as you lift and open your chest. Look toward your "third eye" (see p.27) and hold the position for five full breaths. Inhaling, lift your head. Exhaling, lower your hips to the floor and release your arms. Now perform a half-*vinyasa*.

*This posture strengthens the arms, shoulders and abdomen, opens the ribcage and relaxes the nervous system.*

1

2

# HEAD-TO-KNEE POSTURE
## Janu Sirsasana

1  Begin in sitting ready pose. Inhaling, lift and bend your right leg, cupping the ankle in your left hand. Exhaling, bring your heel to your groin so that the sole of your foot runs along the inside of your left thigh. Your right knee should point out to the side at 90°, with the knee as close to the floor as possible.

2  Inhaling, fold forward over your left leg, taking hold of your left foot (or shin) with both hands. Pull against your grip, extend through your spine and look up.

3  Exhaling, bring your chest closer to your knee and your chin to your shin. Look at the toes of your left foot and hold the position for five full breaths. To finish, inhaling, raise your head and extend your spine. Exhaling, release your hands and straighten your legs. Repeat the exercise on your left side, then perform a half-*vinyasa*.

*This posture stretches the legs; opens the lower back, hips and knees; and stimulates the circulation and urinary systems.*

1

2

3

# SON OF BRAHMA POSTURE
## Marichyasana

1   Begin in sitting ready pose. Exhaling, bend your right knee, bringing your right foot toward your right hip. Align the outside of your right heel with the outside of your right buttock and place your left hand flat on the floor by your left hip. Inhaling, extend your right arm above your head, lengthen your abdomen and look up.

2   Exhaling, fold forward, wrap your right arm around your right leg and bring your hands together behind you. Aim to clasp your left wrist with your right hand. Inhaling, lengthen through your spine and look up.

3   Exhaling, bring your chest toward your left knee. Look at the toes of your left foot and hold for five full breaths. To finish, inhaling, extend your spine and look up. Exhaling, release the posture. Repeat the exercise on your left side, then perform a half-*vinyasa*.

·  *This posture relieves tension in the lower back, cleanses the kidneys, regulates the digestion and eases constipation.*

1

2

3

# BOAT POSTURE
## Navasana

1   Begin in sitting ready pose. Inhaling, lean back and lift
    your legs in front of you, keeping your feet together, toes
    pointed and legs straight (bend your knees if neces-
    sary). Bring your arms parallel to the floor, palms facing
    each other. Extend through your fingers, lift your chest
    and roll your shoulders back. Look at your toes. Hold for
    five full breaths.

2   Inhaling, place your hands flat on the floor, on either
    side of your hips with the fingers pointing forward.
    Exhaling, cross your legs at the ankles and bring your
    knees toward your chest. Pushing down through your
    hands, draw in your abdomen, shorten your torso and
    lift your body off the floor. Inhaling, lower your body to
    the floor and return to position 1. Repeat this exercise
    three to five times before performing a half-*vinyasa*.

*This posture strengthens the abdominals and lower back, and
stimulates the visceral organs – in particular the intestines.*

1

2

# BOUND ANGLE POSTURE
## Baddha Konasana

1 Begin in sitting ready pose. Exhaling, bring both feet in toward your groin with your soles together. Clasp your feet in your hands, relax the muscles in your hips and groin, and allow your knees to drop toward the floor.

2 Inhaling, press your thumbs into your soles just below the ball of each foot and open out your feet, exposing the soles. Use the rotation of your feet to lower your knees further. Lift your chest, roll your shoulders back and lengthen your spine.

3 Exhaling, fold forward over your feet, keeping your spine lengthened and chest lifted. Bend your elbows, using your forearms to place a downward pressure on your thighs. Look at the tip of your nose and hold for five full breaths. Inhaling, sit upright. Exhaling, release the posture before performing a half-*vinyasa*.

*This posture opens the hips, stretches the inner thighs, strengthens the back and improves pelvic circulation.*

1                         2

3

# BRIDGE POSTURE
## Setu Bandhasana

1   Begin in sitting ready pose. Exhaling, lie flat on your
    back, bending your knees and placing your feet flat on
    the floor as close to your buttocks as possible. Keeping
    your heels together, turn out your feet, allowing your
    knees to move apart while maintaining contact between
    the floor and the soles of your feet.

2   Inhaling, place your palms on the floor, thumbs tucked
    beneath your buttocks. Bend your arms and lift your
    torso, supporting your body on your forearms. Arch
    your back and roll your head back on to the floor.

3   Exhaling, fold your arms across your chest, placing a
    hand on each shoulder. Distribute your weight between
    your head, buttocks and feet. Look at the tip of your nose
    and hold for five full breaths. Inhaling, place your fore-
    arms on the floor and lift your head. Exhaling, return to
    sitting ready pose and perform a half-*vinyasa*.

*This posture opens the chest, increasing breathing capacity.*

1

2

3

# ELEVATED UPWARD BOW
## Urdhva Dhanurasana

1 Begin in sitting ready pose. Exhaling, lie flat on your back with your arms by your sides. Bend your knees, placing your feet close to your buttocks, flat on the floor, slightly wider than hip-width apart.

2 Inhaling, grip your ankles with your hands and push upward with your hips, allowing your back to curve. Bear your weight through your shoulders rather than through your neck. Look at the tip of your nose and hold for five full breaths and a sixth inhalation. During the sixth exhalation lower yourself slowly to the floor. Repeat this exercise three times. When you have finished perform seated forward bend (see pp.78–9), holding the posture for ten full breaths. Then perform a half-*vinyasa*.

*This energizing posture develops the strength and flexibility of the whole body, particularly the spine, legs, buttocks, arms, shoulders and upper back. It also stretches the front of the legs and abdomen, and opens out the chest and shoulders.*

1

2

Withdraw in meditation from the pleasures
of sense as a tortoise withdraws its limbs.
Through this will you find peace.

BHAGAVAD GITA (6TH CENTURY BCE)


Compose yourself in stillness
Draw your attention inward
And devote your consciousness to the Self.
For the wisdom you seek lies within.

BHAGAVAD GITA (6TH CENTURY BCE)

# Chapter Five

# the finishing sequence

The Finishing Sequence is a vital component of any Ashtanga practice, however short, and should be neither rushed nor skipped. The sequence is composed of a number of inverted postures (in which the body is turned upside-down) together with some balancing counterposes. Inverting the body results in an increased supply of oxygenated blood to the head. This enhances brain function, improving our sensory awareness and enabling us to think more clearly and effectively, with greater concentration.

Each posture is held for longer than in previous sequences and the rate of the *ujjayi* breathing is slowed. This serves to return the body to a state of internal equilibrium as the muscles relax, cellular respiration slows, the uptake of oxygen from the blood decreases, the heart rate lowers and the body temperature begins to cool.

Throughout the sequence you should maintain *ujjayi* breathing. However, as you progress through the postures allow each breath to become longer and more relaxed, until finally you resume normal breathing in corpse posture (see p.108).

The postures of the Finishing Sequence should leave you feeling relaxed and refreshed. They are perfect for doing either on their own or together with some sun salutations after a busy day at work.

# SHOULDERSTAND/PLOUGH POSTURE
## Salamba Sarvangasana/Halasana

1  Exhaling, lie down with your arms by your sides. After five long breaths, inhale as you press your arms into the floor, lift your legs and roll up on to your shoulders.

2  Bend your elbows and use your hands to support your back. When you feel stable straighten your legs, pointing up through your toes and drawing in your abdomen to support your back. Look toward your toes or the tip of your nose and hold the position for ten long breaths.

3  Exhaling, bring your feet to the floor behind you, keeping your back upright and legs straight. Then place your arms flat on the floor and interlock your hands. Look toward your abdomen or the tip of your nose. Hold this position for ten long breaths. Inhaling, separate your hands, using them for support as you return your legs to position 1. Exhaling, roll out of the posture.

*This rejuvenating posture stretches and strengthens the upper body, stimulates circulation and improves digestion.*

1

2

3

# FISH POSTURE/EXTENDED LEG POSTURE
## Matsyasana/Uttanapadasana

1 Begin by lying on your back, legs outstretched. Inhaling, place your hands next to your buttocks, bend your elbows and raise your upper body on to your forearms.

2 Exhaling, arch backward, allowing your head to relax back on to the floor. Open your chest, lengthen through your abdomen and point your toes. Look toward your "third eye" and hold the posture for ten long breaths.

3 Supporting your weight with your head and lower body, release your arms as you exhale, extending them over your torso with the palms together. Keeping your legs straight and your feet together, lift them off the floor, pointing your fingers toward your feet. Look at the tip of your nose and hold for ten long breaths. Inhaling, return your forearms to the floor and raise your head. Exhaling, lower your torso and legs to the floor.

*A counterpose to shoulderstand, this posture relieves upper back tension and opens the chest, shoulders and neck.*

1

2

3

# HEADSTAND
## Shirhsasana

1 Inhaling, kneel down. Place your forearms on the floor in front of you and touch each elbow with the fingertips of the opposite hand. Exhaling, without moving your elbows, rotate your forearms outward and interlock your fingers to form a triangle-shaped foundation. Place the crown of your head on the floor between them. Inhaling, straighten your legs, lifting your hips upward.

2 Exhaling, walk your feet toward your head. Inhaling, support your weight through your arms and shoulders as you lift your feet off the floor, bending your knees.

3 When you feel confident, straighten your legs as you exhale, pointing your toes, drawing in your abdomen and pushing down through your forearms. Look at the tip of your nose and hold for up to twenty long breaths. Lower your legs to the floor during the final exhalation.

*This important posture strengthens the arms and shoulders, and floods the brain with oxygenated blood.*

1                  2                  3

# POSE OF THE CHILD
## Balasana

Pose of the child is a counterpose to headstand and balances the effects of the inversions. It is also a classic yoga resting pose, which you can adopt at any point in your practice when you need a break. Based on the fetal position, pose of the child is extremely calming and nurturing, and is useful if you are experiencing any difficult emotions – whether in your yoga practice or in your life generally. Begin by kneeling upright on the floor. Gently sit down on your heels, keeping your spine straight. Allow your arms to hang loosely at your sides and relax your hands. Exhaling, fold forward from your hips, bringing your chest to rest on your thighs and your head toward the floor, ahead of your knees. Let your hands slide backward toward your feet and your arms rest on the floor. Close your eyes and, keeping your breathing soft, even and relaxed, remain here for at least ten breaths (or half the time spent in headstand, if that is greater than ten breaths).

# CROSS-LEGGED POSTURE
## Padmasana (modified)

1 Begin in sitting ready pose. Inhaling, bring first one foot then the other in toward your groin, splaying your knees. Reach behind your back and cup your elbows with your hands. Exhaling, fold forward to the floor. Look to your "third eye" and hold for up to ten long breaths.

2 Inhaling, sit upright. Exhaling, place your hands just behind your hips, palms down with the fingers pointing forward. Inhaling, arch your back and lift your chest. Roll your head gently backward. Look toward your "third eye" and hold for up to ten long breaths.

3 Inhaling, sit upright. Exhaling, place your wrists on your knees, joining the thumbs and forefingers. Draw in your abdomen and lift through the crown of your head. Look at the tip of your nose and hold for up to ten long breaths. Exhaling, release the pose.

*This meditative pose opens the hips, improves posture and circulation, and stills the mind and body to aid focus.*

1

2

3

# CORPSE POSTURE
## Savasana

Always allow yourself time to perform this posture at the end of your practice. It will help to still your mind and realign your body, balancing the effects of the different postures in the sequences. Exhaling, lie down on your back with your arms by your sides, legs outstretched with the feet hip-width apart. Open your arms, turning your palms upward to help your chest open fully. Allow your feet to fall out to the sides. Make any adjustments necessary to ensure that your body is symmetrically aligned and you feel totally comfortable. Returning to normal breathing, close your eyes and relax, allowing the ground to support you as your body sinks into the floor. Focus on the different parts of your body in turn, beginning at your feet and moving toward your head. Work to dissolve any remaining tension. Finally, centre your mind within your body by bringing your attention to the relaxed rhythm of your breath. Remain in this position for at least five minutes.

Above: the heavens – sky, sun, stars, moons, planets.
Below: the elements – space, air, fire, water, earth.
From these: the body – shape and form, vital breath,
digestive fire, blood and water, skeleton and flesh,
And the senses – hearing, touch, sight, taste, smell.
In contemplation of these sets of five,
The wise discovered that all things are holy.
One can complete the inner with the outer.

TAITTIRIYA UPANISHAD (7TH CENTURY BCE)

# ashtanga living

As we have seen, the initial aim of Ashtanga yoga (particularly of the Primary Series) is to cultivate a strong and supple body and a clear and focused mind through the practice of postures and controlled breathing techniques. It is often these elements that attract students to Ashtanga in the first place. However, achieving physical health is really only one aspect of yoga. Practising some of the other limbs outlined in Patanjali's *Yoga Sutras* (see p.12) is the key to introducing Ashtanga into all areas of our lives, both at home and at work.

Patanjali's eight limbs of yoga can be divided into two groups: the external limbs of *yama* (ethics), *niyama* (self-discipline), *asana* (posture practice) and *pranayama* (controlled breathing); and the internal limbs of *pratyahara* (withdrawal of the senses), *dharana* (concentration), *dhyana* (meditation) and *samadhi* (enlightenment or union with the true self).

In this chapter we begin with a discussion of the external limbs – the outward attitudes and practices that we should adopt toward ourselves, others and our surrounding environment. Once we have understood these, we can take our first steps on the more meditative path of yoga when we learn about the internal limbs, which take us on a journey of self-discovery and spiritual transformation.

# THE EXTERNAL LIMBS

The external limbs of yoga involve physical effort and the conscious training of the mind and body in preparation for the internal limbs. In addition to *asana* and *pranayama* (discussed in previous chapters), the external limbs consist of *yama* and *niyama*, which are concerned with our personal, social and ethical attitudes and modes of behaviour.

## Yama ethics

*Yama* is the first external limb and comprises five moral guidelines that teach us how to conduct our relationships with others and our environment. The first guideline is *ahimsa*, meaning nonviolence. This requires us to adopt an attitude of compassion toward all living things. Traditionally *ahimsa* involved the practice of vegetarianism, but today we can also understand it as a general attitude of respect to both ourselves and the world around us. Cultivate *ahimsa* in your yoga practice – remember to listen to your body with respect for your limitations; guard against the temptation to force your body into postures that are beyond its capabilities.

The second *yama* is the attitude of *satya* or truthfulness. Total honesty demands great courage but it is important to remember that telling a lie, however small, undermines our sense of worth – not only in the eyes of others, but more importantly in our own eyes, too.

*Asteya* (nonstealing) is the third *yama* and involves asking for no more than we need. For example, we should avoid taking anything, be it time, energy or wealth, from others unless it is freely given.

The fourth *yama* is *bramacharya*. Traditionally this was interpreted as the practice of chastity. Today we can understand it as a more general instruction to exercise moderation and self-restraint in all aspects of our lives.

*Apariggraha* is the fifth *yama* and means nonattachment or nonpossessiveness. A common pattern of human behaviour is to resist change by holding on to things, such as desires, people or material possessions, in an attempt to generate confidence and security. However, this state of being prevents us from living in a free and vital way. Instead it is better to welcome change, viewing it as an opportunity for growth and learning.

### Niyama self-discipline

*Niyama* is the second external limb, comprising five principles that focus the mind on the inner quest for enlightenment. The first *niyama* is *sauca*, which means cleanliness or purity. *Sauca* refers not only to the cleanliness of our bodies, but also to our internal health. To practise *sauca* try to limit some of the toxins that you habitually ingest – not only alcohol and tobacco, but also the additives in processed foods, the pesticides sprayed on fruit crops, and the chemical residues in tap water.

The second *niyama* is *samtosa* (contentment). To achieve *samtosa* we need to focus our attention on the positive things that bless us in the present. This feeling of gratitude leads us to an automatic sense of abundance that we experience as contentment. Practising the meditation on p.118 will help you to experience this *niyama*.

The third *niyama* is *tapas*, which translates literally as "fire" or "heat". To live with an attitude of *tapas* is to demonstrate burning enthusiasm and commitment in all that we do – from mundane chores, such as cleaning the kitchen, to more challenging tasks, such as meeting deadlines. By channelling our energies in this way, we become more effective and feel happier as a result.

The fourth *niyama*, *swadhyaya*, means self-study. *Swadhyaya* involves developing awareness of our inner selves – of the unconscious urges that affect our behaviour and the beliefs that limit us – in order to expand our potential as human beings. To develop this *niyama* take time to reflect on your relationship with your yoga practice. What attitudes do you bring to each posture? You will probably find that they mirror your attitudes to life as a whole. This awareness is the first step to change.

The last of the *niyamas* is *ishwara-pranidhana*, which means devotion to a higher being or source of energy. If you are religious you can practise this *niyama* by worshipping the god of your chosen faith. Otherwise simply take some time to reflect in reverence and thanksgiving on the wonder of the world that surrounds you and the miracle that is your life.

# CREATING CONTENTMENT

This visualization exercise will help you to develop *samtosa* (contentment) in your life. Practise it in the morning before rising – it will improve your mood for the rest of the day.

1   Sit or lie in a comfortable position on the floor with your back straight. Half-close your eyes and soften your gaze.
2   Consider the word contentment. What does it mean to you? How does it manifest itself within you – in your thoughts and feelings?
3   Think of a time in the past when you have experienced contentment. Perhaps while walking the dog, enjoying the warmth of sunshine in spring, or spending time with loved ones. Imagine yourself in that moment now, allowing the feelings of contentment to wash through you, filling your mind and permeating your body.
4   Allow your memories to drift away, but hold on to the sense of contentment that you have generated. When you feel ready, return your awareness to the present.

# THE INTERNAL LIMBS

Once we have gained control over the mind and body by practising the external limbs of yoga, we are ready to develop yoga's internal limbs – *pratyahara*, *dharana*, *dhyana* and *samadhi*. These represent four stages of an inward journey toward spiritual enlightenment – the discovery of a point of stillness within the self and union with the universal consciousness.

**Pratyahara** withdrawal of the senses
*Pratyahara* is the first step on the road to meditation as we shift our attention from our external world, experienced through the senses, to our inner world. In Ashtanga yoga the *drishtis* (gaze points; see p.27) help us to develop this limb: by focusing on fixed points we limit what we can see around us.

**Dharana** concentration
When we are able to focus fully on the inner self, without becoming distracted by thoughts, emotions or the

activities of others, we achieve the state of *dharana*. Practise the simple meditation on p.123 to help you to develop this limb.

## Dhyana meditation

*Dhyana* describes a deep meditative state in which we lose the sense of separateness between being and doing. For example, when practising the *vinyasas* of Ashtanga yoga we reach *dhyana* when we become so absorbed in our practice that we experience self, movement and breath as one.

## Samadhi union with the true self

Translated literally from the Sanskrit, *samadhi* means the "peace that passes all understanding". *Samadhi* is the highest meditative state – the point of "yoga" or "union" at which the yogi is said to have reached spiritual enlightenment. In this state any remaining sense of a separate self dissolves altogether as the yogi experiences oneness – a complete sense of connection to the universe and all that it contains.

# DEVELOPING DHARANA

Practise this simple meditation exercise at the end of your yoga session — it will help you to develop the concentration of *dharana*, freeing your mind from distractions and drawing your attention inward. Build up your meditation practice slowly. Start with ten minutes and increase the duration when you feel ready.

1 Sit in a comfortable position on the floor or on a chair, with your back straight and your eyes closed.

2 Focus each one of your senses on the physical action of breathing: listen to the rhythmic, rushing sounds of each inhalation and exhalation; feel the air on your skin as it passes in and out of your nostrils; experience the gentle expansion and contraction of your chest cavity; visualize each breath as it flows in and out of your lungs.

3 If you experience any distracting thoughts, do not feel frustrated. Simply observe each thought without judgment as it passes through your mind. Then return your attention to the breath once more.

When we live our lives with passion we crusade for
our hearts: we dare to hope and to dream, without
fearing failure; we are inspired with great purpose,
our thoughts boundless and our minds open to
embrace a world of limitless possibilities; hidden
talents and abilities awaken in the face of challenge
and excitement; and we discover ourselves to be greater
people by far than we ever imagined we could be.

PATANJALI

YOGA SUTRAS (C.200BCE–C.200CE)

# INDEX

# PICTURE CREDITS AND ACKNOWLEDGMENTS

Picture Credits

The publisher would like to thank the following people, museums and photographic libraries for permission to reproduce their material. Every care has been taken to trace copyright holders. However, if we have omitted anyone we apologise and will, if informed, make corrections in any future edition.

**Page 13** Makoto Saito/Photonica; **26** Mieko Kanasachi/Photonica; **33** Getty/Image Bank; **37** Yukari Ochiai/Photonica; **49** Steve Bloom Images; **73** Getty/Stone; **95** Getty/Stone; **109** Getty/Stone; **111** Getty/Image Bank; **119** Getty/Image Bank; **122** Getty/Image Bank; **125** Getty/Stone

Author's Acknowledgments

I dedicate this book to all of my teachers along my path so far, especially my first teachers: Francis, my mum; William, my dad; Michael and Sarah, my family. Kate – thank you for your heart, your kindness and your unwavering faith and support on the yoga path. Sarah and Nigel – thank you for the miles of smiles and just for being there. Lois – you taught me so much, how can I ever thank you enough? There are no words … . Ross and the class of '88, we had the best of times. For precious moments and special lessons I thank in no particular order: Wendy, Ambro, Lino, Louly, Catherine, Nick and Helena, Barty, Angela, Russ and Caron, Noonie and Jiggster, to name but a few. For all my students, you continue to be my teachers and my inspiration. See you on the mat sometime.
Love and hugs, may peace and light be with you all, always.
*OM Shanti Namaste*
Anton ×

Publisher's Acknowledgements
Model: Kate Moore
Make-up artist: Tinks Reding